D0214836

WITHDRAWN
UTSA LIBRARIES

WITHDRAWN
UTSA LIBRARIES

Botswana:
An African Growth Economy

LIBRARY
The University of Texas
At San Antonio

Other Titles in This Series

LIBRARY
The University of Texas
At San Antonio

Westview Special Studies on Africa

Botswana: An African Growth Economy
Penelope Hartland-Thunberg

When Botswana achieved full independence in 1966, informed opinion was unanimous in assessing the country's economic prospects as dismal. Ten years later, Botswana celebrated a decade in which its real economic growth averaged a remarkable 15 percent annually, its infrastructure was expanded, three new cities and a number of new industries were established, and government revenues increased ten times over. This miracle of growth was wrought by an aggressive development plan based on private enterprise and foreign investment, aided by generous allocations from foreign aid donors, and directed by skilled and devoted leaders working within an environment of political stability.

Dr. Hartland-Thunberg deals both factually and analytically with the economic success of Botswana, basing her work on the most recent official data. She also includes government regulations and official policy statements regarding foreign investment in Botswana. Her work makes a unique and much needed contribution both to development literature and the African studies field.

Penelope Hartland-Thunberg is currently director of economic research at Georgetown University's Center for Strategic and International Studies. She previously served as a senior staff member for the Council of Economic Advisors and as a commissioner for the U.S. Tariff Commission. She has also taught at Brown University, Mount Holyoke College, and Wells College.

Botswana:
An African Growth Economy
Penelope Hartland-Thunberg

Westview Press / Boulder, Colorado

Westview Special Studies on Africa

All rights reserved. No part of this publication may be reproduced or transmitted in any form or by any means, electronic or mechanical, including photocopy, recording, or any information storage and retrieval system, without permission in writing from the publisher.

Copyright © 1978 by Westview Press, Inc.

Published in 1978 in the United States of America by
    Westview Press, Inc.
    5500 Central Avenue
    Boulder, Colorado 80301
    Frederick A. Praeger, Publisher

Library of Congress Cataloging in Publication Data
Hartland-Thunberg, Penelope.
    Botswana: an African growth economy.
    (Westview special studies on Africa)
    Includes index.
    1. Botswana—Economic conditions.
HC517.B6H37   330.9'68'103   78-3477
ISBN 0-89158-171-5

Printed and bound in the United States of America

Contents

Tables

Preface

Botswana as an economy or even as a country is an unknown quantity in the United States. It is tiny and underdeveloped; it has commanded no headlines because of political or racial strife. Its economic orientation is primarily toward the rest of southern Africa and Europe. Those Americans who have any firsthand acquaintance with it are largely big game hunters and anthropologists. Expertise on the economy of Botswana in the United States is confined to a few specialists (usually British) from the International Monetary Fund and the World Bank. Research on the economy of Botswana in this country is a practical impossibility.

This monograph is a first approach toward filling the information gap. The bulk of the information on which it is based was collected during my visit to Botswana as a consultant for the U.S. Agency for International Development in the fall of 1976. At that time, official and private U.S. interest in southern Africa was just awakening from a period of hibernation. Since then, interest in the area has continued to grow and seems certain to mount.

Despite its size and obscurity, Botswana merits attention. During its first decade of independence, it became one of the few success stories in black Africa, in terms of both economic development and political stability. The reasons for its achievements are worth studying because its success is unique and was accomplished despite seemingly overwhelming odds. Botswana's strengths have, until recently, been ignored, but they stand in stark contrast to conditions in the rest of black Africa and to the enormous obstacles against which it has had to struggle. It is a remarkable and commendable country from which important precepts can be drawn. This study attempts to summarize them.

Penelope Hartland-Thunberg

Statistical Note

The data presented in this monograph have been taken almost exclusively from official sources—from publications of the Botswana government or from conversations with officials. Where a nonofficial source is used, it is cited.

Until late 1976, when Botswana created its own currency—the pula—the South African rand was accepted as legal tender and used as the unit of account. During the transition period, when both the pula and rand were circulating, the two currencies were exchanged in the ratio of one-to-one. The rand is, therefore, used throughout this monograph. In the period I cover, the value of the rand in U.S. dollars varied on the average as follows:

Year	One Rand Equals
1969–1971	$1.40
1972	1.30
1973	1.44
1974	1.47
1975	1.36
1976	1.15

In mid-1977 the pula appreciated in value in terms of the rand and the dollar, being set at $1.20 while the rand remained at $1.15.

REPUBLIC OF BOTSWANA

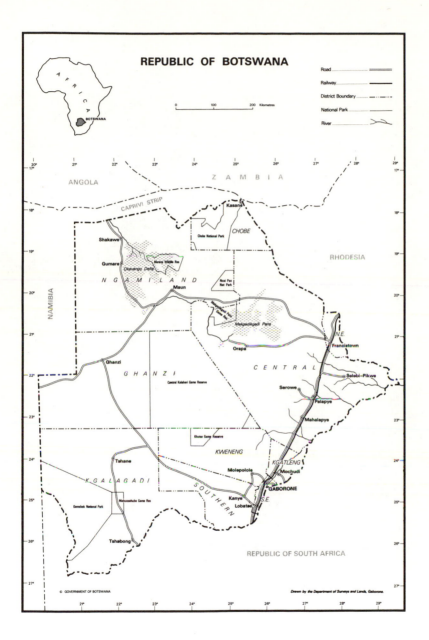

Road
Railway
District Boundary
National Park
River

0   100   200   Kilometres

AFRICA
BOTSWANA

ANGOLA
ZAMBIA
CAPRIVI STRIP
Kasane
CHOBE
Chobe National Park
RHODESIA
Shakawe
Moremi Wildlife Res
Gumare
Okavango Delta
N G A M I L A N D
Maun
Nxai Pan Nat Park
Makgadikgadi Pans
NAMIBIA
N.E.
Orapa
Francistown
Ghanzi
C E N T R A L
G H A N Z I
Central Kalahari Game Reserve
Selebi–Pikwe
Serowe
Palapye
Mahalapye
Khutse Game Reserve
Tshane
KWENENG
KGATLENG
Molepolole
Mochudi
K G A L A G A D I
Kanye
GABORONE
Gemsbok National Park
Mabuasehube Game Res
SOUTHERN
Lobatse
S.E.
Tshabong

REPUBLIC OF SOUTH AFRICA

© GOVERNMENT OF BOTSWANA

Drawn by the Department of Surveys and Lands, Gaborone.

1. Introduction

Botswana is a country of sharp contrasts. It is both large and small, rich and very poor, modern and traditional, changing and changeless. Above all, it is a tranquil, soft-spoken, harmonious society surrounded by bloodshed, bigotry, and mounting civil strife. The analogy to the eye of a hurricane, widely cited in Botswana, is apt.

Botswana is about the size of Texas, but has fewer than 700,000 people. Recent and continuing exploration has revealed previously unknown deposits of raw materials—diamonds, copper, nickel, coal, salt, potash, and soda ash—but the per capita income is just over $400. Modern industry employs people who frequently live in traditional, picturesque villages with widely scattered whitewashed roundavels. Gross domestic product (GDP) has recently been growing at more than 15 percent a year, but on weekends people leave the cities and towns to visit their cattle on distant traditional ranches.

The Batswana are in fact eight main tribes, all of which speak the same language, Setswana, although English is the official tongue. These tribes are mercifully free of the traditional tribal animosities that so frequently rend other African nations. They are a gentle, hospitable people, with much natural dignity, and typically evoke a warm reaction in foreigners.

The country celebrated the tenth anniversary of its independence on September 30, 1976. But before it became the Republic of Botswana, it was the British Protectorate of Bechuanaland. The protectorate was established in 1885 with some reluctance, because Cecil Rhodes claimed that it was the "Suez Canal to the north." In 1909, when the constitution of the proposed Union of South Africa was being discussed, Bechuanaland, Botsutoland (now Lesotho), and Swaziland asked that they *not* be made part of the new union, and in fact they remained under the protection of Britain. Local tribal government in Bechuanaland evolved into a Legislative Council established by the Constitution of 1961; subsequent proposals for self-government and then independence were accepted and made effective in 1966.

The years of British rule were essentially a period of neglect—benign, as it developed. The people of the area, the Batswana, had originally requested British protection against the Boers of the Transvaal. Protection was granted by the British in part to preclude an eastward push by the Germans who were at that time colonizing southwest Africa. The British never attempted colonization of Bechuanaland, because of its arid climate and the greater attractions of settlement and resource development in South Africa and Rhodesia. The fact that Botswana had no real colonial history probably helps explain the present interracial harmony existing in Botswana, its lack of bitterness toward the white industrial countries, and its present white population, as well as its pro-Western orientation.

The country is a parliamentary democracy headed by the widely respected president, Sir Seretse Khama. In the late 1940s, the young Seretse, son of a tribal chief and grandson of the greatly revered Khama the Great, shook the foundations of the Protectorate when, as a student in London, he took a white British bride. Despite a long period of exile, the couple persevered in their attempts to return and eventually were invited to do so. Seretse later became head of state upon the death of an uncle in 1959. Sir Seretse is the leader of the Botswana Democratic Party, which has won every election since the one that preceded independence, and is in no way threatened by any of the three small opposition parties. The government is apparently free of graft and corruption and, guided by the firm leadership of Khama, has managed the affairs of Botswana efficiently and rationally for ten years.

Given the misfortune of geography, this has been no simple chore. Botswana is totally landlocked, surrounded by, if not hostile, at least uncordial, white governments. Rhodesia lies to the northeast; south and west is South Africa, with Namibia (Southwest Africa) and the Caprivi Strip on the west and north. At the single point in the north where the Caprivi Strip, Botswana, and Rhodesia all meet, there is also a point of contact in the Zambesi River with Zambia.

The hard facts of geography have totally dominated the economic development of Botswana. The country is a vast Precambrian tableland, much of it covered by the sands and grassy areas of the Kalahari Desert in the southwest. In the northwest the remarkable inland delta of the Okavango River creates the extensive Okavango Swamps. The best agricultural land and highest rainfall are found in the east, where the bulk of the population is located.

In addition, the most direct route between the two main colonial interests of Britain in southern Africa, Rhodesia and the Cape Colony, happened to lie through this populous eastern section of what became Botswana. It was along this eastern strip of land that the railroad, intended to connect the two colonies and to extend from the Cape to Cairo, was built. The accident of this railroad's location has been of crucial importance to the economic development of the Republic of Botswana.

The existence of this modern link to the outside world (especially to the booming economy of South Africa), the discovery of new deposits of mineral wealth, and the growing export market for beef (its most traditional commodity) brought unexpected prosperity to the new republic in its first decade. Gross domestic output, which had been virtually stagnant during the postwar years, leaped forward; exports and imports mushroomed, and the foundations of a modern, thriving economy were put in place. The boom of the late 60s and early 70s was given pause by the quantum jump in the price of petroleum in 1974, the subsequent worldwide recession, and mounting political turmoil in Botswana's two white-controlled neighbors. The relative impact of these events is difficult to judge.

The future is uncertain and will depend on events largely beyond the control of the country—on economic developments in world markets and on the degree of political turmoil in neighboring countries. The Batswana, however, are hopeful and are not without certain advantages. The following pages describe the present structure of Botswana's economy, analyze the main forces acting on it, and discuss its strengths and weaknesses.

2. The Structure of the Economy: Aggregative Trends

In the mid-1960s, Botswana was receiving from Britain a substantial annual subsidy (up to R9 million). Most believed that its continuation to at least 1980 would be essential for balancing the new government's accounts. Indeed, a Ministry of Overseas Development (ODM) Survey Mission reporting in 1966 (the Porter Report) took a very dismal view of the country's prospects for economic development. It saw agriculture as the only feasible source of growth and agreed that continued foreign subsidies would be necessary for more than a decade. The economy had no infrastructure worthy of the name; it had only 54 miles (90 kilometers) of tarred roads, no real communications or power network, and an unreliable water supply. Private surveyors had located deposits of diamonds and copper, but the future of mineral development seemed bleak because of the enormous costs of developing an adequate infrastructure.

Nonetheless, by 1976 the subsidy had been discontinued because it was no longer necessary. Botswana had become self-supporting; it was meeting its recurrent budget and 40 percent of its development budget (see Appendix Table A.8). Three new cities had been started and urbanization was growing at about 15 percent a year. The country had more than

1,000 kilometers of tarred roads, a country-wide telephone network, and was completing an integrated power system in the populous eastern section. Between 1971 and 1976, real growth averaged 10 percent annually, well in advance of the 2 to 3 percent increase in the population. Between 1968 and 1975 growth averaged nearly 20 percent a year.

The miracle was wrought by an aggressive development program based on foreign investment in mineral extraction. A diamond mine had been opened and was operating; a copper-nickel mine and refinery had finally conquered a series of unforeseen problems and were achieving full output; a coal mine was providing an increasing proportion of the country's fuel requirements.

In contrast to some of its black-governed neighbors, the Republic of Botswana has always vigorously supported private ownership and operation of business and encouraged foreign investment. Mineral surveys have been undertaken almost exclusively by private companies, although the government has done some test drilling.

Government encouragement of foreign investment in private enterprise was unquestioned until 1974. In that year the basic diamond mining agreement with the DeBeers Corporation was renegotiated under terms much more favorable to Botswana. Since then, concern has been voiced within the local corporate community over the country's commitment to private investment and its willingness to continue to encourage investment by foreign companies.

How much the complaints of the business community were motivated by posturing for bargaining position and to what degree potential foreign investors were deterred by the renegotiation of the DeBeers agreement is difficult to judge. The decline in foreign investment in Botswana in 1975 and 1976 was at least partially a consequence of the worldwide decline in investment and the depressed state of world markets for raw materials. It was also probably traceable in part to heightened racial tensions in neighboring Rhodesia and

South Africa, on whose economies Botswana's economy so crucially depends.

In addition, the commitment of the Khama government to the policy of encouraging foreign investment has never been unanimous. The most ardent advocate of the policy has been the Ministry of Finance and Development Planning, the predominant ministry for, though not the sole formulator of investment policy. Khama himself, although strongly oriented toward Western capitalism, is also an astute politician. The government does require public participation in major undertakings that are of strategic economic importance for the country. When invited by the two local commercial banks to participate in their operations, however, the government refused the opportunity.

Government Policy

A basic motivating force behind Botswana's push for economic development has been, and continues to be, its desire to lessen its dependence on South Africa. The dominant influence of the South African economy upon almost every facet of Botswana's economic life has been dictated by geography, history, and the enormous difference in size between the two countries. According to any measure—population (26 million versus 0.7 million), land area (471,000 square miles versus 232,000), gross domestic product (R19 billion versus 0.19 billion in 1973)—Botswana is a midget and South Africa a giant. Moreover, history and proximity to South Africa left Botswana with a patrimony of almost complete economic integration in the South African economy. So thoroughly had Botswana become absorbed into the South African economy that it was not until 1972 that Botswana began to collect data on foreign trade. After a decade of independence, estimates of Botswana's balance of payments existed in only rudimentary form. Though the achievement of relative economic independence is a major task, progress has been made.

In pursuit of greater economic independence, Botswana has replaced the South African rand, which was legal tender in Botswana for the first decade, with its own currency, the pula. It has sought export markets outside of southern Africa and has been especially successful in marketing its beef in Europe. By 1976, probably two-thirds to three-quarters of Botswana's trade was with South Africa, compared to four-fifths before that time. The government has announced its intended takeover of the only railroad in the country, which is owned and operated by Rhodesian Railways, and it has made a start in establishing commercial and business services in Botswana (e.g., wholesale establishments and insurance and finance companies), thereby avoiding total reliance on South African sources.

During the first decade, however, massive South African investment in the development of Botswana's mineral resources served to increase the country's ties with its giant neighbor. Botswana was a member of the Southern Africa Customs Union, which was dominated by South Africa but administered more equitably as a result of Botswana's protests. During these early years, nearly half of all Batswana in gainful employment were working in South Africa and returning R 1–2 million annually to Botswana.

The prospect of supplying cash employment in Botswana for these 40,000 people in the foreseeable future, however, is slight. Botswana is attempting to achieve a greater measure of economic independence by diversifying its trade relations and increasing "localization" of business ownership, management, and the labor force. Botswana has three other important planning goals: first, rapid economic growth at a sustained average rate of 10 to 15 percent annually; second, a more equitable distribution of income and wealth and educational opportunity in order to equalize the opportunity for advancement; and third, high investment returns in mining and industry, which will be reinvested in education, agriculture, labor-intensive manufacturing, and local services.

Botswana's economic success to date is traceable to a favorable world economic climate, a very efficient planning organization, and aggressive, dedicated government leadership. The planning and financing of development are combined in one ministry, the Ministry of Finance and Development Planning (MFDP). There, a system of "indicative planning" for the public sector is coordinated by the cabinet and a group of able and dedicated senior civil servants, many of whom are European expatriates. General policy directives given by the cabinet are translated into sectoral priorities through spending guidelines for the departments. These guidelines are derived from the careful calculation of revenues likely to be generated by plan fulfillment. Planning for the private sector is by inference only.

Much care goes into the entire planning and financing process. Actual expenditures in the recurrent budget have been approximately equal to planned targets year after year. The fact that the planning and financing of development are implemented in tandem has contributed to the ability of the planning process to meet development goals within the confines of the budget.

The Planning Ministry works in five-year cycles, drawing up a five-year indicative plan that is revised ("rolled over") every three years. In 1976, work on the fourth National Development Plan (NDP IV) was completed after discussions with cabinet and ministry officials and presented to the legislature for final approval late in the year. The first plan, NDP I, covered the years 1967 to 1972; NDP IV spans 1976 to 1981. The overlapping five-year planning intervals, which encompass plan adjustments after three years of experience, have contributed to the success of the planning process.

Diversification of economic activity has been encouraged by the Botswana Development Corporation (BDC), a government-owned company established in 1970 to aid in financing new business ventures in all sectors of the economy except mineral development, which the government encourages directly. Initially, BDC assumed control of business interests that the government had acquired—e.g., minority share-holdings in a game lodge, hotels, a shopping complex—and later participated in a wide variety of small business enter-prises, including manufacturing, business services, and whole-sale trade. It has relinquished its ownership participation whenever private investors could be found to take its place. Supported by funds from the government's budget, its assets amounted to about R9 million in 1976. Altogether, it held an interest in 31 companies (concentrated in the field of com-mercial and financial services) and had created more than 4,000 jobs.

Botswana's remarkable growth rate resulted from the allocation of 50 percent or more of gross domestic product to investment. With high investment and high growth, imports increased more than 700 percent between 1966 and 1975; government revenues, which are derived primarily from import duties and fees and secondarily from income taxes, increased more than 1,000 percent. Enormous domestic investment was supplemented by substantial inflows of foreign capital, both public (foreign aid programs) and private. (See Table 2.1.)

During the first decade, the main agent of growth was the mineral industry. Exploitation of mineral resources was emphasized in the planning process and actively pursued by government officials. Mining development involved compli-cated negotiations and financing arrangements; it also involved sizeable expenditures, financed by government loans, to improve the infrastructure. The bulk of the water, power, and transport facilities necessary for opening the new mines was provided by the government. As a result of mineral ex-ploitation and the associated infrastructure construction, GDP grew at a rate of 20 percent a year in real terms between 1968 and 1975, and the share of mining and construction in GDP increased from 1 to 12 percent. At the same time,

TABLE 2.1
INCREASE IN NATIONAL AGGREGATES, 1966-1975a
(R million and percent)

AGGREGATES	1966	1971/2	1973/4	1974/5
GROSS DOMESTIC PRODUCT (R million)	36.8	103.6	198.4	205.7
GROSS FIXED CAPITAL FORMATION (R million)	8.1	53.1	77.5	56.8
(Percent)	22.0	51.2	41.0	27.6
IMPORTS OF GOODSb (R million)	18.8	50.7	104.0	119.6
GOVERNMENT REVENUES (Recurrent)c (R million)	6.2	17.1	40.7	60.7
GOVERNMENT FOREIGN BORROWING (R million)	3.7	12.1	27.7	20.2

aAccounting year 1 July-30 June; calendar year for 1966.
bNet of customs duties.
cFinancial year 1 April-31 March.

the share of agriculture declined from 45 to 25 percent. (See Table 2.2.)

Three major mine construction operations were initiated and completed between 1966 and 1976—large-scale diamond mining at Orapa, copper-nickel production and refining at Selebi-Pikwe, and some coal mining at Morupule. In addition, fairly extensive resource surveys revealed a variety of economically exploitable deposits, including soda ash, salt, potash, sodium sulphate, additional copper, gold, iron, and manganese.

The enormous influence of mining and mining interests in Botswana is illustrated by the fact that in 1973/4 GDP was little more than the aggregate cost of commissioning the mine and the surface treatment plant at Selebi-Pickwe

TABLE 2.2
INDUSTRIAL ORIGIN OF GDP AT CURRENT MARKET PRICES, 1965-1976/7
(R million)

Industrial Sector	1965	1966	1967/8	1968/9	1971/2	1973/4	1976/7
1. Agriculture, forestry, hunting, fishing	11.1	14.5	18.3	23.2	34.2	70.1	75.8
2. Mining, quarrying, prospecting	0.2	0.0	0.7	0.2	11.2	15.9	36.7
3. Manufacturing	3.8	2.9	3.6	2.8	5.1	10.1	16.2
4. Water, electricity	0.2	0.3	0.3	0.3	1.3	3.3	7.7
5. Building construction	2.1	2.1	2.0	1.9	10.0	21.1	18.1
6. Wholesale and retail trade, restaurants, hotels	6.2	6.8	5.0	5.1	17.5	34.6	64.2
7. Transport, storage communication	2.7	3.0	2.4	3.4	3.8	5.3	9.1
8. Banking, insurance, real estate, ownership of dwellings, business services	2.1	2.4	2.9	3.5	5.3	13.1	24.3
9. General Government	{ 4.5	{ 4.9	7.7	9.5	11.9	18.2	31.5
Household, social, community services			1.0	1.3	3.5	6.7	15.1
TOTAL GDP	32.8	36.8	43.8	51.2	103.6	198.4	298.7

(R180 million). As mineral development and the associated construction activity progressed, Botswana's exports increased from less than R11 million in 1966 to R105 million in 1975. Mineral products accounted for R54 million. Imports, the main source of government revenue, increased from R19 million to nearly R160 million. The effect on employment, however, was not proportionate; formal sector employment (i.e., employment in the cash economy, which excluded those self-employed in traditional farming and ranching) increased from 48,000 in 1972 to over 60,000 in 1976. In that year, mining accounted for more than 12 percent of GDP, but employed only 7 percent of the cash labor force in Botswana.

Because of the capital-intensive nature of mineral development and its relatively small impact on total employment, in 1976 the Botswana government appeared to be ready to shift the emphasis of planning goals to the rural sector of the economy. Indeed, after the completion of mine construction in 1974, development resources were increasingly directed toward the Accelerated Rural Development Program (ARDP). In Botswana, as in other developing countries with rapidly growing economies, migration from rural areas to "urban" communities increased faster than employment opportunities in those communities and was accompanied by mounting social problems there. In 1976, urban slums had not yet assumed the size or rate of growth that they had achieved elsewhere, but they had become a source of concern in Botswana. The amenities and expanding economic opportunities of centers like Gaborone attracted rising numbers of settlers from the villages. In addition, residents of villages located within commuting distances of employment centers, such as Molepolole, twenty-five miles northwest of Gaborone, sought cash employment there while remaining village residents.

A development program emphasizing labor-intensive opportunities and income distribution rather than maximum government revenue would spread the rewards of development more widely at the cost of a lower growth rate. It would mean stressing the goal of social justice more heavily than the other development goals of rapid growth and conversion of wealth below the ground into income-producing, self-renewing assets above the ground.

The new emphasis in NDP IV on the rural sector will entail more investment in agriculture, education, and the rural infrastructure (e.g., electrification, water, feeder roads). Capital expenditures in these sectors will absorb over half the total allocation for the plan period. It is hoped that they will have the added advantage of retarding, if not reversing, the flow of people from the country to the urban areas.

The Traditional Sector

Botswana is among the least developed countries of the world (and recently protested a U.N. reclassification from the "least"—per capita income less than $201—to the "next-to-least"—per capita income $201–$400—category of development). Nonetheless, the relative importance of the market sector of the economy is large and pervasive. It has been estimated that about 70 percent of total consumption in the country is derived from cash income; the remainder is derived from subsistence income. Moreover, even the very lowest income groups of the rural population derive 30 percent of their income in cash. (It is reported that the legendary bushmen, renowned for their shyness and self-sufficiency, are also beginning to seek part of their income in cash.)

The population is concentrated in the east, where about 80 percent live in a belt along the railroad line. The soils there are more fertile and the rainfall higher than in the west. The pervasiveness of the cash economy is indicated by the fact that only 15 percent of the country's population live in townships, that is, the five "urban" areas of Gaborone, Francistown, Lobatse, Selebi-Pikwe, and Orapa. The remainder live primarily in native villages, with 5 percent of the population employed in South Africa.

Traditional village life is based on crop cultivation and cattle ranching. Most families have three homes—one in the village, one on the farm, and another at the ranch—and move from one to another depending on the season. When the spring rains begin, they move from the village to the ranch, where they tend the cattle. They also drive some of the cattle to the farm—frequently at a considerable distance—for plowing. The main crop is sorghum, but cattle herding is the predominant activity. In 1976, the cattle population was about 3 million, having doubled since 1965, and cattle comprised about 10 percent of the country's capital formation.

Cattle play a special role in the life of the average Batswana. They are a source of wealth and power, a source of food, and the object of a preferred way of life. Those who do not own their own cattle usually tend someone else's. Cash employment is often sought in the urban areas in order to make possible the purchase of cattle. On weekends many city dwellers leave for their ranch to tend their cattle. As one European, a longtime resident of Botswana, observed, "The Batswana *love* their cattle."

Land cultivation is not held in the same high esteem as ranching. Sorghum is the main crop, but maize, largely imported, is replacing sorghum as the main food-grain. Because maize cultivation requires more rainfall than sorghum, it is not a reliable crop in Botswana, although increasing amounts are being grown. Sorghum, however, requires more labor for cultivation (because of its vulnerability to birds) and for milling (in order to remove bitter seeds). The consumption of sorghum has declined as more people have sought employment in townships.

One-third to one-half of the basic foodstuffs consumed in Botswana are imported. In fact, the only two processed foods that the country does not need to import are beef and honey; 50 to 60 percent of the food-grains are imported, depending on the size of the harvest.

The dividing line between the traditional, self-sufficient sector of the economy and the modern, cash-interdependent sector has become increasingly blurred. Even the most affluent households derive 30 percent of their income in kind, that is, through an increase in the number of their cattle. For middle-income households, 40 to 50 percent of their income takes the form of agricultural production or an increase in the cattle herd. Most villages have at least one store that sells the basic necessities—maize meal, sugar, tea, soap, and matches (all, except maize, entirely imported)—as well as some canned foods. In addition, itinerant traders with hawkers' licenses distribute the basics in more remote areas. Households often brew and sell beer for cash.

The shift away from traditional village life is illustrated by the fact that only about 2.5 percent of the population lived in townships in 1964, in contrast to 8 percent in 1971, and 15 percent in 1976. In the interim, three new towns were created—Gaborone, the new capital, and Orapa and Selebi-Pikwe, two mining centers. By 1976, Gaborone had become the largest "urban" area, with over 37,000 people; the largest villages were Serowe, with 40,000, and Mahalapye, with 38,000.

The Modern Sector

The vast expansion of Botswana's economy during the first decade of independence, when the average annual increase in total output (GDP) amounted to more than 15 percent, was partly illusory. As is frequently true for developing countries, Botswana's statistical competency improved during the period of rapid growth. Enhanced statistical reliability and coverage account for some of the apparent growth. The Central Statistics Office estimates that about 25 percent of the growth in GDP between 1971/2 and 1973/4 was the result of statistical illusion, but that such statistical growth ceased to be a problem in the totals after 1975.

In addition, annual price increases estimated at 12 to

15 percent after 1970 imply that the estimates of real growth are less reliable than changes in current prices. Inflation in Botswana has inevitably accompanied inflation in South Africa because of Botswana's close links to the South African economy. The two countries share common external tariffs, a common sales tax, free trade, and a common currency. Thus, prices in Botswana have paralleled those in its giant neighbor; techniques available to Botswana for controlling inflation have been similarly limited.

Despite the inevitable data problems, the rate of economic change in Botswana during the first decade was impressive. Not only was the economy growing rapidly, but its structure was being transformed. As previously noted, agriculture declined while mining rose in importance. At the same time, the building boom that usually accompanies rapid growth caused the construction industry's share of GDP to rise from 6 to 10 percent. The other major sectors of the economy—manufacturing and services (trade, transport, finance)—remained about the same or declined in relative importance, but showed rapid absolute increases.

Table 2.3 shows the changes in the industrial structure of the economy. It should be noted that a serious drought in 1965 depressed the role of agriculture and accentuated manufacturing and services. Indeed, the relative importance of the various economic sectors during these years is more accurately portrayed by the 1966–67 data, when there was less extreme rainfall.

The decline in the relative importance of manufacturing and services occurred despite the sizeable increase in output in absolute terms (see Table 2.2). Thus, manufacturing rose 400 percent and trade rose 1,000 percent in output value, but mining and construction grew, from very low bases, at a much faster rate. Such dramatic and apparently contradictory relative shifts are characteristic of an economy in the early stages of development, when undertaking a single project can cause a quantum jump in GDP.

TABLE 2.3
INDUSTRIAL ORIGIN OF GDP AT CURRENT MARKET PRICES, 1965-1976/7
(Percent)

Industrial Sector	1965	1966	1967/8	1968/9	1971/2	1976/7[a]
1. Agriculture, forestry, hunting, fishing	33.8	39.4	41.8	45.3	33.0	25.4
2. Mining, quarrying, prospecting	0.6	0.0	1.6	0.4	11.0	12.3
3. Manufacturing	11.6	7.9	8.2	5.5	5.0	5.4
4. Water and electricity	0.6	0.8	0.7	0.6	1.3	2.6
5. Building and construction	6.4	5.7	4.6	3.7	10.0	6.1
6. Wholesale and retail trade, restaurants, hotels	18.9	18.5	11.4	10.0	17.0	21.5
7. Transport, storage, communication	8.2	8.2	5.5	6.6	4.0	3.0
8. Banking, insurance, real estate, ownership of dwellings, business services	6.4	6.5	6.6	6.8	5.1	8.1
9. General Government	13.7	13.3	17.6	18.6	11.5	10.5
Household, social, community services			2.3	2.5	3.4	5.0
TOTAL GDP	100	100	100	100	100	100

[a]Estimate.

The role of the government in the economy rose to a peak of over 20 percent in 1968/9 when the infrastructure necessary for the new mineral projects was being established and other smaller initiatives were undertaken. Since then, despite sizeable absolute increases, the share of the public sector in GDP has declined to about 15 percent. The decline was most marked in the area of government construction and administration. This was countered somewhat by the rising relative importance of government-provided social services (health, education, etc.), which represented up to 5 percent of GDP (see Table 2.3).

The composition of national product in terms of functional source (distributive shares) and final expenditures is contained in Tables 2.4 and 2.6. The most noticeable changes are the role of capital formation and the return of capital and land (profits, interest, rent) to management and owners.

The importance of export-oriented investment as an agent of growth and development for Botswana became clear during the first decade of independence. The modern sector of the economy was almost nonexistent in 1965; private consumption accounted for more than 90 percent of GDP, and the country required an annual subsidy from Britain— amounting to nearly 15 percent of total consumption—to balance its accounts. Between 1965 and 1972, when market conditions were extremely propitious for all raw material producers, fixed investment rose 700 percent, while private consumption rose only 200 percent. As a consequence, consumption declined from more than 90 percent to less than 60 percent of total output, and domestic savings rose from less than 5 percent to more than 25 percent of a much larger GDP.

In contrast to the 1960s, when net foreign investment accounted for 85 percent of fixed investment, in the early 1970s the share of foreign capital dropped to about 50 percent, and the role of private foreign capital (as opposed to public foreign capital, mostly on concessionary terms)

TABLE 2.4
GROSS DOMESTIC EXPENDITURE AT CURRENT MARKET PRICES, 1965-1974/5
(R million)

Expenditure	1965	1966	1967/8	1968/9	1971/2	1973/4	1974/5
FINAL CONSUMPTION	37.0	38.1	49.4	54.3	75.1	136.3	158.6
Government Consumption Expenditure	7.9	9.3	11.6	11.3	16.0	28.3	37.0
Private Consumption Expenditure	29.1	28.8	37.8	43.0	59.1	108.0	121.6
Marketed	21.9	19.9	28.2	31.6	35.1	75.0	90.0
Non-marketed	7.2	8.9	9.6	11.4	24.0	33.0	31.6
INCREASE IN STOCKS	- 5.2	- 1.4	2.1	7.3	1.3	26.0	44.8
Cattle, etc.	- 5.0	- 3.8	3.6	6.1	- 0.7	17.4	13.7
Other Stocks	- 0.2	2.4	- 1.5	1.2	2.0	8.6	31.1
GROSS FIXED CAPITAL FORMATION	7.2	8.1	9.9	9.9	53.1	77.5	56.8
Modern Sector	6.0	6.8	na	na	53.0	77.2	na
Traditional Sector	1.2	1.3	na	na	0.1	0.3	na
NET FOREIGN INVESTMENT	- 6.2	- 8.0	-17.6	-20.3	-25.9	-40.3	-48.5
Export of Goods	10.4	10.8	10.2	11.7	39.8	76.4	93.8
Less Imports of Goods[a]	-16.6	-18.8	-27.8	-32.0	-50.7	-104.0	-119.6
Less Imports of Services (Net)	b	b	b	b	-15.0	-12.7	-22.7
NET ERRORS AND OMISSIONS	-	-	-	-	-	- 1.1	- 6.0
GROSS DOMESTIC EXPENDITURES	32.8	36.8	43.8	51.2	103.6	198.4	205.7

[a] Net of customs duties.
[b] Included Under Imports and Exports of Goods

TABLE 2.5
GROSS DOMESTIC EXPENDITURE AT CURRENT MARKET PRICES, 1965–1974/5
(Percent)

Expenditure	1965	1966	1967/8	1968/9	1971/2	1973/4	1974/5
FINAL CONSUMPTION	113.0	103.5	113.0	106.1	72.4	68.7	77.1
Government's Share	24.0	25.2	26.4	22.0	15.4	14.3	18.0
INCREASE IN STOCKS	- 16.0	- 4.0	5.0	14.2	1.3	13.1	21.8
GROSS FIXED CAPITAL FORMATION	22.0	22.0	23.0	19.3	51.2	39.1	27.6
NET FOREIGN INVESTMENT	- 19.0	- 22.0	- 40.2	- 40.0	- 25.0	- 20.9a	-26.3a
GDP	100.0	100.0	100.0	100.0	100.0	100.0	100.0

aIncluding Errors and Omissions.
Detail may not add to total because of rounding.

TABLE 2.6
GROSS DOMESTIC PRODUCT AT CURRENT MARKET PRICES BY SOURCE, 1965-1974/5
(R million)

Source	1965	1966	1967/8	1968/9	1971/2	1973/4	1974/5
WAGES AND SALARIES (Compensation of Employees)	28.9	32.9	13.1	14.5	30.7	68.2	92.6
PROPRIETORS' INCOME Rents and Profits			25.4	31.5	56.7	98.9	76.2
The Modern Sector's Share					26.6	44.5	30.3
The Traditional Sector's Share			na	na	30.1	54.4	45.9
CAPITAL CONSUMPTION	1.9	2.0	2.7	3.0	5.2	15.9	18.1
The Modern Sector's Share					5.0	15.6	17.7
The Traditional Sector's Share	na	na	na	na	0.2	0.3	0.4
INDIRECT TAXES	2.1	2.0	2.6	2.1	11.2	15.4	18.5
Less Subsidies	-0.1	-0.1	-0.0	-0.0	-0.2	-	-
GDP AT MARKET PRICES	32.8	36.8	43.8	51.2	103.6	198.4	205.7

Detail may not add to total because of rounding.

expanded greatly. The breakdown of foreign investment by public and private sources is not available, but a comparison of government borrowing from foreign sources (Table 2.1) and net foreign investment in Botswana (Table 2.4) suggests that private sources accounted for roughly half of the total inflow until the early 1970s. Both imports and exports mushroomed, the former bringing a great expansion of government revenues. This "operation bootstrap" was eminently successful because it was soundly conceived and efficiently executed and because the external modalities were propitious. Whether it can be repeated will depend on circumstances beyond Botswana's control. However, the episode of growth during the country's first decade provides an almost classic example of how a developing country with a determined and devoted leadership can help itself. Tables 2.4 and 2.5 illustrate with uncommon statistical clarity the shifts in the national aggregates accompanying rapid growth.

Tables 2.6 and 2.7 show the impact of the development process on income flows. Wages and salaries as a share of national income changed little until the last years of the decade. This tendency reflects the country's dependence on imported skills and expertise during the construction phase and demonstrates that construction techniques were not labor-intensive. The fact that proprietors' income in the traditional sector was equal to wages and salaries until 1973 shows the importance of village life and the large economic role played by the community-owned land and cattle holdings of the villages. (The privately owned "freehold farms" are included in the modern sector.) Some of the increase in proprietors' income in 1973 reflects the profitable operations of the diamond mine at Orapa; the decline in 1974/5 is traceable to problems at Selebi-Pikwe.

Tables 2.8 and 2.9 show the emphasis on the construction and mineral industries in Botswana's investment policy. These tables also show public investment, or "General Government," not included in such infrastructure sectors as

TABLE 2.7
GROSS DOMESTIC PRODUCT AT CURRENT MARKET PRICES BY SOURCE, 1965-1974/5
(Percent)

Source	1965	1966	1967/8	1968/9	1971/2	1973/4	1974/5
WAGES AND SALARIES	88.1	89.4	30.0	28.3	30.0	34.4	45.0
PROPRIETORS' INCOME			58.0	62.0	55.0	49.8	37.0
CAPITAL CONSUMPTION	6.0	5.4	6.2	6.0	5.0	8.0	8.8
INDIRECT TAXES	6.4	5.4	6.0	4.1	11.0	7.7	9.0
GROSS DOMESTIC PRODUCT	100	100	100	100	100	100	100

Detail may not add to total because of rounding.

TABLE 2.8
GROSS CAPITAL FORMATION AT CURRENT MARKET PRICES BY SECTOR, 1965-1973/4
(R Million)

I.S.I.C. Major Division	Kind of Sector	1965	1966	1967/8	1968/9	1971/2	1973/4
1.	Agriculture	-5.0a	-3.8a	4.2	7.3	0.2	10.8
2.	Mining and quarrying	na	na	0.6	1.9	27.3	26.1
3.	Manufacturing	-0.4b	2.2b	-1.5c	0.8	1.9	-0.9
4.	Water and electricity	na	na	0.0	0.1	10.9	18.6
5.	Building and construction	na	na	0.1	0.2	1.7	3.3
6.	Trade, hotels, restaurants, etc.	0.2b	0.2b	1.0	0.7	1.8	6.7
7.	Transport and communication	na	na	1.5	0.7	2.5	2.5
8.	Finance, real estate, insurance, and business services	1.2	1.3	1.6	1.7	0.8	7.1
9.	Household and community services, etc.	na	na	0.0	0.2	1.6	1.4
	General Government	5.3	6.0	4.5	3.6	7.0	17.0
	Unallocated	0.7	2.6	-	-	-	-
	TOTAL	2.0	8.5	12.0	17.2	55.7	92.6

a Cattle only.
b Stocks only.
c Stocks were reduced by 2.2 million during 1967/8.

TABLE 2.9
GROSS CAPITAL FORMATION AT CURRENT PRICES BY SECTOR, 1965-1973/4
(Percent)

I.S.I.C. Major Division	Kind of Sector	1965	1966	1967/8	1968/9	1971/2	1973/4
1.	Agriculture	-250.0	- 45.0	35.0	42.4	0.4	12.0
2.	Mining and quarrying			5.0	11.0	49.0	28.2
3.	Manufacturing	- 20.0	26.0	-12.5	5.0	3.4	- 0.9
4.	Water and electricity			0.0	0.6	19.5	20.1
5.	Building and construction			0.8	1.2	3.0	3.5
6.	Trade, hotels, restaurants, etc.	10.0	2.3	8.3	4.1	3.2	7.2
7.	Transport and communication			12.5	4.1	4.5	3.0
8.	Finance, real estate, insurance, business services	60.0	15.3	13.3	10.0	1.4	8.0
9.	Household and community services			0.0	1.2	3.0	1.5
	General Government	265.0	71.0	37.5	21.0	12.5	18.3
	Unallocated	35.0	31.0				
	TOTAL	100	100	100	100	100	100

Detail may not add to total because of rounding.

transport and water. (Construction of roads and railroads appears under the transport sector; construction of dams and aqueducts appears under the water sector.) Investment in mining and construction was negligible in 1965 and 1966; after that it mounted rapidly. By 1971/2, when the project at Orapa was nearing completion, mining accounted for one-half of gross investment. Its share dropped precipitously after that, in part because favorable grazing conditions and high world prices for beef encouraged an expansion of the cattle herd. The capital formation contained under the heading "General Government" includes the establishment of the new capital at Gaborone, where Parliament and the major ministries are housed in a specially designed quadrangle, which was completed in 1970. The jump in 1973/4 includes expanded government expenditures, primarily operating costs.

The accelerating effect of massive investment on the economy appears in the rise of investment in such sectors as trade (6) and finance (8) to accommodate the increasing consumer and business demand for goods and services. Favorable weather conditions and rising incomes of villagers and freehold farmers have encouraged the increased investment in agriculture. The devastating effect of a drought in 1965, which forced the premature slaughter of cattle, explains the low investment figure for agriculture in that year, when gross capital formation amounted to only R2 million.

3. The Crucial Role of the Transportation Sector

Transport and Development in Botswana

A transportation system is the necessary prerequisite for the development of specialization and exchange in an economy. Botswana's single railroad, originally built by the British to join the British Cape Colony with Rhodesia, has been instrumental in generating and sustaining the growth of Botswana's economy. It permitted the development of industry along its length, and it stimulated the marketing of the products of traditional industry at home and abroad. Without it, the economy today would be little more than a collection of self-sufficient households existing at subsistence level and relying extensively on a barter exchange.

Although the relative importance of the railroad has declined in recent years, it still accounts for about three-quarters of the tonnage of freight originating or terminating in Botswana. The remainder of the freight movement is by road; movement of freight by air or water is negligible in terms of tonnage. Passenger movement by rail still apparently predominates, but a lack of data on road passengers leaves its relative importance ambiguous.* The rapid growth in the

*Informal movement of passengers by truck, sometimes for lengthy distances, is a common practice throughout the country.

gross product of the air sector in recent years reflects the lack of available alternatives for long-distance passenger traffic in the country. Air traffic, however, plays only a minor role in total transport activity.

Thus, the transportation sector is overwhelmingly dominated by the single railroad—a one-track, 3 foot 6 inch gauge line stretching north-south for 641 kilometers along the eastern edge of the country. It brings in the bulk of Botswana's essential foods, fuels, and manufactured goods, and carries out the beef and minerals that pay for them. The railroad is owned and controlled by foreigners; Botswana has no railroad assets, except for the land on which it is built.* It has no railway operating expertise, provides no railroad maintenance, and collects no railroad operating information. Rather, it relies on Rhodesian Railways, which operates through its territory, to provide all these services.

The Botswana track extends from Ramatlabama on the South African border to Vakaranga on the Rhodesian border in the north and represents more than 20 percent of the total mileage of Rhodesian Railways. The line through Botswana is managed from Bulawayo in Rhodesia as part of the Southern District of Rhodesian Railways. Trains operate between Bulawayo and Mafeking, which is 25.9 kilometers from the Botswana border in South Africa. An agreement between South African Railways and Rhodesian Railways provides the latter with running rights. South African Railways does all the making-up and marshaling at Mafeking; Rhodesian Railways does the same at Bulawayo. There is no marshaling yard in Botswana where trains can be reformed. There are no service or maintenance facilities, except for a mobile maintenance and repair unit sent in from Bulawayo in case of an

---

*Botswana now owns two recently completed branches, aggregating 75 kilometers, that connect the coal mine and copper mine to the main road.

emergency. No administrative, managerial, or staff functions are located in Botswana.

The line uses diesel electric locomotives, which are capable of hauling 1,000 tons and 110 axles, and 4-axle "bogie" freight cars. The average freight train contains twenty to twenty-two cars carrying 700 to 750 gross tons. The capacity of the line is thought to be ten to eleven trains per day, although Rhodesian Railways provides no information on this subject. An upgrading of the main line rails from Bulawayo through Botswana was completed in late 1976.

The decline in the relative importance of the transport sector in total output (Table 2.3) is due not only to the rapid growth of other sectors, but also to financial losses incurred in recent years by the entire Rhodesian Railways system. The operating surplus of R0.6 million in 1967/8 on the Botswana section dropped to a deficit of R2.1 million in 1973/4, thereby virtually wiping out any contribution by railroad transport to the net output (value-added) of the sector. The gross output of the railroad, however, increased by 60 percent between the two periods (Table 3.1). The volume of traffic originating in, or destined for Botswana increased both relatively and absolutely, but about 80 percent of the freight carried by rail in Botswana still represents transit traffic between South Africa and Rhodesia (Table 3.2).

Road transport is provided by both the public sector— through the Central Transport Organization (CTO)—and the private sector. Because data on the latter are undoubtedly incomplete, estimates of value-added and volume of output overstate the importance of the public sector and understate the importance of road transport in the total economy. The CTO is the government department responsible for maintaining and operating the entire government fleet of motor vehicles, which represents a sizeable portion of the total motor vehicles in the country.

There were fewer than 18,000 motor vehicles registered

TABLE 3.1
COMPARISON OF PRODUCTION ACCOUNTS FOR RHODESIA RAILWAYS
IN BOTSWANA, Years 1967/8 to 1974/5 (R million)

Inputs	1967/8	1968/9	1971/2	1973/4	1974/5
Intermediate Consumption	8.3	8.0	11.0	16.2	na
Compensation of Employees	0.9	0.9	1.2	1.5	na
Depreciation[a]	0.6	0.6	0.7	0.9	na
Indirect Taxes	0.0	0.0	0.0	0.0	na
Operating Surplus	0.6	1.8	0.0	-2.1	na
Total: Gross Output	10.4	11.4	12.9	16.5	na
Value Added	2.1	3.3	1.9	0.3	na

[a]Depreciation on rolling stock is not included. This follows
an international statistical convention, where rolling stock,
depreciation, etc., is counted in the "head-office" country
only.

in Botswana at the end of 1976. Approximately 13 percent
were CTO vehicles. In 1975, trucks and passenger cars each
accounted for 25 percent of all privately-owned vehicles.
Light delivery vans represented another 20 percent, and
8 percent were tractors. Buses, motorcycles, and other vehicles
comprised the remainder. It is estimated that about 60 percent of the country's motor vehicle capacity is unavailable
because of inadequate repair and maintenance facilities and
a lack of qualified mechanics.

Most of Botswana's trucks have small hauling capacities.
The country relies on South African trucking concerns for
large-scale hauling. The ready availability of competitive
foreign trucking services has permitted Botswana to maintain

TABLE 3.2
RAILROAD TRANSPORT WORK DONE IN BOTSWANA, 1971-1976

Passengers carried, by class	1971/2	1972/3	1973/4	1974/5	1975/6
1st	13,918	13,369	17,351	16,603	17,197
2nd	50,337	57,492	58,877	59,037	63,643
3rd	211,386	222,630	226,692	96,864	101,002
4th	364,616	418,139	366,524	397,660	380,393
TOTAL	640,257	711,630	669,444	570,164	562,235

Freight in million net ton/km	1971/2	1972/3	1973/4	1974/5	1975/6
Intra Botswana	na	26.5	33.6	37.2	na
Export	na	5.8	10.8	14.2	na
Import	na	77.4	112.1	130.3	na
Other	na	834.1	774.0	875.6	na
TOTAL	997	943.8	930.5	1,057.3	na

only average-demand trucking capacity, thus reducing the amount spent on road transport equipment. The use of imported services to handle peak load needs probably costs Botswana far less than it would cost to maintain a fleet of heavy-duty tractor-trailers with considerable average excess capacity.

Botswana's rudimentary road network reflects the sparsity of the population. For example, there are only 50,000 people in the west, an area larger than California. The entire country is the size of France or the state of Texas (220,000 square miles), but it has fewer than 700,000 people. The fact that about 80 percent of its residents live within 50 miles of the railroad means that, except in the east, roads are little more than lightly traveled tracks through the bush and desert.

The sparsity of the population and the low average income level in the country means that the road network bears little traffic. The light traffic justifies only the expenses required for dirt or gravel roads without chemically treated surfaces. As a result, surface travel throughout the country—except for the north-south road paralleling the railroad between Lobatse and Francistown in the east—is slow, hazardous for vehicles without 4-wheel drive, often arduous, and in some seasons impassable in many places. Clearly one of the reasons for the sparsity of the population in the west, north, and south is that these parts are isolated and inaccessible. There is little reason to make them more accessible, however, until demand for better transport facilities increases substantially. Better farming or ranching opportunities, or mineral development in these areas could provide such justification. So would rapid economic growth across the borders in Namibia, Zambia, Rhodesia, or South Africa, if accompanied by appropriate public policy measures, for Botswana is a hinterland for sections in all of these countries. At present, however, political considerations and economic stagnation in these neighboring areas have precluded any changes in transport patterns.

Public policy since independence has favored the expansion and upgrading of the entire road network. Botswana views this as the best way to expand the transport infrastructure and to lessen the country's strategic and economic dependence on a foreign-owned and -controlled source of transport. Air transport has been neglected—one official said "starved of funds"—because it is a mode of transport available only to the upper income groups. (Income distribution in Botswana is highly unequal, and in 1974, 45 percent of all families were earning less than the Poverty Datum Line—a standard that provides the bare necessities according to family size. Government policy has tried to raise the lowest income group by providing expanded employment opportunities and better social services for them.) But the most recent plan for air transport (NDP IV) includes an airport capable of accommodating intercontinental jets and the upgrading of several airfields. Even so, capital expenditures for civil aviation account for only 12 percent of the combined road and airport programs, although air transport has generated 16 percent (1973) of the combined output of the two sectors.

The national airline, Air Botswana, which is owned by the Botswana Development Corporation, provides only flight bookings and aircraft handling on the ground. It is licensed to operate scheduled services in Botswana, but subcontracts its routes to Air Service Botswana Ltd., a subsidiary of a South African concern, which provides the actual operations in the air. In addition, South African Airways and Zambia Airways provide scheduled service into Botswana. The total scheduled traffic is about equally divided between Air Botswana and the two foreign airlines. Several small private companies also operate a growing charter business within Botswana.

Plans for the Transportation Sector

Botswana's extreme dependence on a foreign-owned corporation colors and shapes its plans for the future development of the transportation network. Botswana only grudgingly retains economic relations with Rhodesia and refuses to conduct formal diplomatic relations with that country. To lessen this strategic and economic vulnerability, Botswana has announced a policy of eventual nationalization of the railroad. The vagueness of Botswana's plans for taking over the railroad are a reflection of the enormous economic and technical difficulties it confronts in implementing such a policy. Its current five-year plan, NDP IV (1976–1981), for example, contains no measures aimed at railroad nationalization. Botswana officials are engaging in somewhat indefinite discussions with the Rhodesian Railways on "localization."

The "Botzam road" project calls for the upgrading of the link between Francistown and Nata and the construction of a gravel road from Nata to Kazangula, the only point on the northern border where ferry service provides a connection between Botswana and Zambia. Botswana government officials have given the project top priority among current planning goals. Widely referred to in Botswana as "our lifeline," this project was at its inception the country's sole defense expenditure. Botswana hopes that it will also have beneficial economic consequences in the north and northwest sections.

Until mid-1977, Botswana had no armed forces and undertook no "defense" activities in the usual sense. Its police force was responsible for both maintaining internal order and policing its boundary areas to prevent guerrilla activities in the country. Botswana maintains a neutral position toward such activities, but offers sanctuary to all bona fide refugees. It has adopted these policies in order to survive in the "eye of the hurricane." In its foreign policy Botswana has staunchly supported majority rule in neighboring countries. Its president, Sir Seretse Khama, is one of the "frontline" leaders attempting to coordinate policies on developments in southern Africa. Botswana has been rigorous in maintaining its position of territorial neutrality.

Such a policy, of course, acknowledges Botswana's position as a landlocked country without a self-sufficient economy. The chapter on foreign trade describes Botswana's dependence on South Africa for all essentials and for a route to the sea. If its South African borders were closed, suffering in Botswana would be widespread and intense.

Its economic dependence on Rhodesia, however, is not nearly as great and centers on Rhodesian ownership and operation of its single railroad. Because of its strategic vulnerability, Botswana was accorded a special dispensation from the U.N.-sponsored embargo of Rhodesia. Trade between the two countries continues but its volume and composition are uncertain.

Thus far, militant black groups in Rhodesia, Zambia, and Mozambique have not interfered with the operation of the railroad. But the Botswana government is concerned that this situation may change. In fact, mounting tensions between the white Rhodesian government and black guerrilla groups in neighboring countries, involving frequent violations of Botswana's territorial neutrality by both whites and blacks, forced the country to undertake the formation of a defense force in mid-1977.

The Botzam road project, which would provide a connection to Zambia, seems particularly important because it would insure Botswana access to the outside world if its other borders were closed. The project could properly be viewed as a defense expenditure that might also bring sizeable economic benefits, although its economic justification, per se, was debatable—and debated. The official attitude was that the road expenditures were also justified on economic grounds because the road would open the northwest to economic development—tourism, farming, ranching—and provide an artery for trade between South Africa and Zambia. Others were skeptical. They argued that big game hunters would be more likely to seek air routes than road transport, that farming possibilities were limited by light rainfall and lack of irrigation, and that the delicate ecological balance would easily be upset by overgrazing. In addition, they argued that much of the potential trade between South Africa and Zambia was too bulky to move economically by road, and that when the rail connection between the two countries (through Rhodesia) was reestablished, it would divert whatever traffic might in the interval have moved over the Botzam road.

The arguments have merit, but they are based on different assumptions. Events will determine which argument is correct. If the road is paved, and if the ferry link to Zambia across the Zambesi River is replaced by a bridge, the cost differential between road and rail transport will be lessened, thus encouraging more trade to move by road. As a result, the cost of living, as well as input and marketing costs in the northwest would be lessened, and economic opportunities would expand. Also, if political instability continues in Rhodesia or South Africa, rail transport might seem unsafe. If the road is more heavily traveled, more services will spring up along the road because investment in such establishments will be considered more likely to be profitable. And, if rising copper prices bring prosperity to Zambia and alleviate its current balance-of-payments deficit, it might buy some of Botswana's beef supplies. Finally, there is always the possibility that new strains of grain will be developed that will be more suited to growing conditions in Botswana and provide more food and export materials.

Unless these factors materialize and unless the world demand for minerals improves, the Botzam road will lack both political and economic justification. The most important assumption is the duration of political instability. The longer it lasts, the more justification there will be for the road. It is unclear whether the 1976-1977 interlude will lead to political settlement or intensified turmoil. Thus, Botswana must wait to make its final decisions. But the road has been upgraded, and the European Development Fund has agreed to provide the funds for a tarred surface.

Although air transport has been growing rapidly and the country has many landing strips, only three are paved. The largest airport at Gaborone cannot accommodate international jet traffic. Although plans exist for the construction of an international airport at Gaborone, only its site has been made specific. No studies on its optimum size have been done.

4. Agriculture

Although its importance has diminished, agriculture remains the largest single industry in Botswana, accounting for about one-third of GDP. Because of the arid climate, agricultural output is highly dependent on weather conditions. The relative importance of the agriculture sector in Botswana's economy varies considerably between years of drought and years of favorable weather. In the east and north, rainfall averages about twenty-one inches annually; in the west it averages nine inches or less.

Cattle raising remains the dominant agricultural activity. Cattle account for about 80 percent of the marketed agricultural output and for 55 percent of total agricultural production. Crops comprise 20 to 25 percent of agricultural output. In traditional villages, most crops are produced for the farmers' own use. Traditional hunting, forestry, and fishing activities produce the remaining agricultural output.

Land tenure is of two types, freehold and traditional. Traditional land tenure includes farms on either tribal or state lands. There are about 400 freehold farms operated by about 300 farmers, farming partnerships, companies, or trusts in the various freehold "blocks." The most prosperous of these is the Tuli Block in the east along the Limpopo River border with South Africa. In the east, freehold farming is mixed, but livestock production dominates crop output; in the west, freehold farming is exclusively cattle raising. Not all freehold farmers own their own land; some lease, some are tenants, and some are in the process of buying their land from the government. Freehold farms are typically large and prosperous. They represent the most important source and form of wealth among the Batswana and white farmers in upper income brackets.

The traditional, or non-freehold, farmers in Botswana's rural areas number about 65,000. These farmers have their permanent residences in the tribal villages, but spend a sizeable part of the year in farming areas and at grazing sites. Most Batswana are small cattle producers and subsistence farmers who produce crops and milk mainly for their own consumption. There are, however, enormous differences in production and wealth, but a few very wealthy farmers are included in the traditional category. The top 10 percent of the farmers own more than 50 percent of the cattle in the non-freehold sector, while 23 percent of the rural population and 45 percent of the rural households own no cattle. In the 1971/2 season, 50 percent of the sorghum farmers produced less than 20 percent of the sorghum harvested.

As noted in Chapter 2, sorghum is the main crop, although maize (corn) is being grown in increasing quantities. (Crop production data, however, are not available.) The shift to maize is a source of concern to the authorities because it is an unreliable crop in an arid climate. Officials believe that a reversal or retardation of the movement of villagers to the townships would halt or slow the replacement of sorghum by maize. They see this as desirable because it would limit the increasing dependence of Botswana on imported food supplies.

As much as 50 percent of the food-grains consumed in Botswana are being imported, according to reliable estimates; in fact, 33 to 50 percent of all basic foodstuffs (including oil, sugar, and tea, as well as grains) are imported. By both value and volume, maize is Botswana's most important imported food. Some is imported in the form of meal, but most is imported as grain and milled in Lobatse. The Lobatse mill buys both local and imported grain, and its maize meal is widely distributed all over the country. In good crop years the mill purchases 75 to 80 percent of its grain on the local market; in drought years as little as 20 percent is local product. In contrast, the country is self-sufficient in sorghum in most years, with most of the grain being laboriously milled by "hand" (actually, by foot) in the villages by the farmers.

Inadequate crop storage facilities have contributed to wide price fluctuations for both producers and consumers. A bumper sorghum crop in 1973/4 and lack of storage capacity depressed prices in that year and in 1974/5. This price collapse caused the government to intervene in sorghum pricing through an emergency purchasing program by the recently established Botswana Agricultural Marketing Board (BAMB). The BAMB set a floor price for sorghum and, with the aid of hastily improvised storage facilities, was able to purchase and store grain in the last part of 1974.

Since its initial price stabilizing operation, BAMB has constructed five storage and marketing depots and has extended its activities to maize and other crops. It is hoped that in time the buying and selling activities of BAMB will sufficiently stabilize crop prices to encourage farmers to increase crop acreage for the cash market.

Traditional farming techniques and precarious water supplies combine to keep yields low in Botswana. A prime goal of the Accelerated Rural Development Program is increased yields through improved farming methods. Training centers have been established around the country where courses are given to farmers and their wives; agricultural and extension workers also visit farmers in the fields. Research supporting this extension service is conducted at the Agricultural Research Station, near Gaborone, which is staffed mainly by experts from Britain. The development program also aims to promote industries and crafts in rural areas in order to expand employment opportunities there. Finally, it attempts to augment available social services (education, health, medical, and welfare) in order to contribute to higher standards of living in rural areas.

Botswana is an important cattle-raising and beef-exporting country. Strenuous efforts by the authorities eradicated hoof-and-mouth disease in the mid-1960s. The current policing of borders, a cattle inspection system, and the observance of veterinary fences by cattle-raisers throughout the country have kept Botswana free from that scourge. (An outbreak that forced the closing of the abattoir and the collapse of meat exports in 1978 was the first occurrence in over a decade.) These efforts have paid handsome dividends to the country and the cattle-raisers. Botswana's meat and meat products have been accepted with veterinary approval for some years in the United Kingdom and, more recently, in France. Such veterinary acceptance of its meat by developed industrial countries makes Botswana unusual among the least developed countries. In Lobatse, a modern government-owned abattoir—the largest meat-exporting facility in Africa—sells to Great Britain, South Africa, Switzerland, Austria, Hong Kong, and Zambia.

The movement of cattle to market (the Lobatse abattoir) is primarily by rail because most of the population and agricultural activity are located in the east in a band paralleling the rail line. From ranches in the west, the movement is mainly by truck, although a significant fraction is still "trekked." In order to compensate for the loss of weight that results when cattle are walked to market, and to augment the return per head, the Botswana Meat Commission (BMC) has recently established a network of "fattening" ranches. Preslaughter feeding can substantially increase producers' income.

The cattle population increased at a net rate of about 8 percent during the years 1970–1975, although the size of the herd varied from year to year, depending on grazing and water conditions. In 1976, the country had about three million head of cattle (Table 4.1). The annual slaughter rate, which has remained near 200,000 in recent years, is considerably less than optimum (10 percent of the size of the herd), but it has been limited by slaughtering capacity and tradition.

Because overgrazing of land has already destroyed large pasture areas, the government has introduced a tribal grazing land policy to improve animal husbandry and land tenure. Grazing land is divided into three zones: communal areas where traditional methods will be preserved, commercial areas that will be leased for ranching, and open areas that will be reserved for future use. Because land tenure is such a delicate issue, the government is proceeding very slowly with the new policy.

Most of the commercial processing and marketing of cattle is controlled by the BMC at the Lobatse abattoir. (There are also a few small abattoirs that cater to local consumption requirements.) Despite a sizeable modernization and enlargement program completed in early 1976, officials view the 1200-head-per-day capacity of the Lobatse facility as inadequate for the country's requirements and as a bottleneck to expanded exports.

The BMC purchases cattle directly from large cattle owners, from cooperatives, whose activities account for an increasing proportion of market business, and from traders, who collect cattle into the minimum size lots specified by the BMC. The Commission sets its purchase price by estimating probable beef prices in foreign markets and its own costs.

Exports of meat, meat products, and cattle have more than tripled since 1970, but the consistent annual increases have concealed the turmoil of Botswana's marketing efforts (Table 4.2). Until 1973, sales to the United Kingdom increased dramatically, rising from 40 to 64 percent of total exports. During these years, there were no import restrictions to limit Botswana's sales to the United Kingdom, and rising world beef prices benefited export receipts. After 1973, the shift in the world beef market, the business recession, and the

TABLE 4.1
BOTSWANA: CATTLE POPULATION AND RECORDED OFFTAKE, 1971-1976

Year	Cattle population (end of year)	Slaughtered by BMC	Live Exports	Total recorded Offtake
1971	2,159,000	167,180	250	167,430
1972	2,082,000	156,510	---	156,510
1973	2,276,000	209,647	239	209,886
1974	2,553,000	186,041	282	186,323
1975	2,910,000	188,440	102	188,542
1976	2,855,000[a]	212,000	na	na

[a] June 30, 1976

TABLE 4.2
BOTSWANA: DESTINATION OF MEAT EXPORTS, 1970-1975 (R million)

	1970	1971	1972	1973	1974	1975
Botswana Meat Commission (net sales)						
South Africa	4.5	4.9	5.1	4.6	23.6	na
Other Africa	1.9	3.1	2.5	4.1	3.6	na
United Kingdom	4.8	4.9	10.2	20.0	5.6	na
Other Countries	0.8	2.1	2.1	2.5	1.5	na
TOTAL	12.0	15.0	19.9	31.2	34.3	37.2
Of Which:						
Beef Carcasses (net sales)						
South Africa	3.2	3.3	3.8	3.5	11.5	na
Other Africa	1.2	1.7	1.1	0.3	----	na
TOTAL	4.4	5.0	4.9	3.8	11.5	na
Boneless Beef (net sales)						
South Africa	0.4	0.6	0.4	0.6	7.9	na
Other Africa	0.3	0.8	1.0	3.2	3.2	na
United Kingdom	4.5	4.0	4.6	17.6	5.4	na
Other Countries	0.4	1.7	1.4	1.5	1.4	na
TOTAL	5.6	7.1	7.4	23.0	17.9	na

United Kingdom's entry into the Common Market (which itself was stockpiling beef to support European farm incomes) greatly reduced Botswana's British export sales. In 1974, the United Kingdom's share of BMC sales fell from 64 to 16 percent. Because the South African economy reacted more slowly to these developments, Botswana was able to market its beef there at a good price, and the South African share rose from an average of 15 percent to 69 percent in 1974.

The European Economic Community (EEC) and the African, Caribbean, and Pacific (ACP) countries signed the Lomé Convention Agreements early in 1975. These agreements removed the EEC ban on beef imports from ACP countries, but subjected them to the EEC's prohibitive variable import levy. Negotiations aimed at reducing the levy were immediately undertaken. Botswana's situation became urgent because of quota limits on the flow of beef to South Africa. In mid-1975, Botswana and the other ACP beef exporters obtained a 90 percent reduction of the levy for six months and Botswana's exports returned to 1973 patterns. The agreement was later extended for additional six-month intervals through 1976. Then, late in 1976, after much protesting, the community agreed to a twelve-month quota for 1977. Meanwhile, Botswana has attempted to diversify its export markets, but balance-of-payments problems in South Africa, Zambia, and other neighbors have limited export opportunities in those countries.

5. Mineral Industries

The motivating and sustaining force of mineral exploration and development in Botswana's rapid economic growth has been noted frequently in earlier chapters. This development centered on diamonds, copper-nickel matte, and coal. Diamonds and copper-nickel matte were produced exclusively for export markets; coal was produced for domestic consumption. By the end of 1976, diamond mining and coal mining had become successful economic ventures, but the copper-nickel enterprise had not yet become profitable.

Copper-Nickel Development

Copper was discovered in the Shashe area in the northeast in 1967. The government immediately began planning a mining and industrial complex there, which was to be fully integrated into the economy. At Shashe, fifty miles away, a dam was built to provide water for the complex and for parts of the relatively populous northeast. A coal-powered generating station was constructed as part of the Botswana Power Corporation's (BPC) plan to provide power for the complex and the surrounding area. The refinery was designed to produce copper-nickel matte and elemental sulphur. Local materials, such as sand and silica, bricks, and cement blocks, were used whenever possible.

From the beginning, the project was plagued by a continuing series of technical problems, many of which should have been foreseen by the operating company. These difficulties caused enormous cost overruns. As a result, the mine and treatment plant cost more than twice the original estimate of R95 million, and the operating company was forced to assume a heavy burden of debt.

The mine finally achieved capacity production—3,500 tons of matte a month—in late 1976. According to a long-term contract, it is shipped to the American Metals Climax (AMAX) Port Nickel refinery in Louisiana for further processing and eventual sale to the Federal Republic of Germany. The operating company, Bamangwato Concessions, is owned jointly by Botswana Roan Selection Trust Ltd. (Botswana RST), which holds 85 percent control, and the Botswana government. Botswana RST is in turn owned by AMAX and the Anglo-American Corporation/Charter Consolidated Group. (Each corporation has about 30 percent of the equity.)

Because of the technical problems, associated delays, and extra expenses, the financial situation of the Botswana RST through 1976 was bleak. The collapse of the world price of copper and nickel after 1973 also contributed to the company's problems. The sales contract was based on prevailing prices on the London Metal Exchange. Low prices there, as well as higher operating costs, resulted in an operating loss in 1975 (exclusive of the financing charge on loans for the year). In 1976, operating costs were covered due to rising output and rising metal prices, but revenues were not sufficient to contribute to overhead. It seems likely that the mining operation will remain marginal; it will be able to meet its costs only when world metal prices are close to cyclical highs. More efficient management, however, could compensate for some of the high cost of operation. Most important in determining the future profitability of the mine is the world price of nickel. The mine produces copper and nickel in about equal amounts, but the unit price of nickel has historically been about three times that of copper.

Coal Development

The colliery at Morupule, southwest of Selebi-Pikwe, was built to provide coal for the smelter and the power plant at Selebi-Pickwe and to meet the Botswana Power Corporation's coal requirements in the Gaborone area. It was designed to produce only 200,000 tons a year from an open-pit operation, although the country's coal resources would allow higher production levels. Coal reserves are already estimated at 4 billion tons, and the country has not yet been thoroughly surveyed. Botswana hopes to find coking-quality coal, for which there is a buoyant market around the world; its known coal deposits are of low quality. The high sulphur content makes the coal appropriate only for steam or fuel uses.

The full output from the Morupule mine is consumed at Selebi-Pikwe and Gaborone. The power supply in the capital was primarily based upon diesel oil until 1974, when construction started on a steam-based power station. By the end of 1976, three-quarters of the power requirements of Gaborone were satisfied by steam-generated power from coal. The older diesel facilities were available for peak loads.

Morupule is fifteen miles from the main rail line between Lobatse and Francistown. Botswana constructed a feeder line from the colliery to the main railroad and from the latter to Selebi-Pikwe to provide for coal transport. Coal from Morupule also moves south to Gaborone by rail.

Diamond Development

In contrast to the problem-plagued copper mine, the diamond mine at Orapa in central Botswana fulfilled even the most optimistic expectations. In mid-1971, production of industrial-quality diamonds began. Some high-quality gem stones were also obtained. With the exception of an access road constructed by the government, the project was developed entirely by DeBeers through its subsidiary, DeBeers Botswana Mining Company, Ltd., of which it owns 85 percent. The access road was constructed with funds loaned to the government by DeBeers, which were repaid within five years. A new town was constructed at Orapa to provide homes for 2,600 people employed there. The mining company also constructed a reservoir, which is fed by water from the Okavango area, an electrical power plant, and a small airfield to accommodate the planes used to transport the diamonds to London. In addition, DeBeers participated in establishing the Botswana Diamond Valuing Company (BDVC). Fifty-five percent of the BDVC is owned by the Botswana Development Corporation. The new corporation trains Batswana in diamond-sorting and diamond-marketing techniques at the London headquarters of the DeBeers Central Selling Organization.

The DeBeers' exploration program also resulted in the discovery of diamond-bearing pipes in the south of the country at Jwaneng. A large-diameter drilling program was initiated. Forty percent of the output from the new mine was estimated to be of gem quality, compared to only 13 percent from Orapa.

From the beginning, the Orapa venture was profitable for the company and the government. In 1975, after a long period of negotiations between DeBeers and the government, a new agreement was reached concerning production at Orapa and development of the two new Kimberlite pipes twenty-four miles southeast of Orapa. The government's share in the ownership of the mining company increased from 15 to 50 percent. A new tax structure gave Botswana 65 to 70 percent of the profits from Orapa and the new operations, in the form of taxes, royalties, and dividends.

The consequences of the sharply higher tax rate imposed

on DeBeers were controversial. DeBeers' marginal, 15 percent rate of return seemed to imply that DeBeers had agreed to operate a management contract in Botswana. Many business-men in Gaborone claimed that these terms would discourage further private investment in the country. Foreign private investment did decline after 1975, but other conditions had also changed. Investment worldwide was depressed by the prevailing business recession, and political instability in Rho-desia and South Africa created risks for export-oriented investment in Botswana. Others in the Gaborone business community contended that DeBeers had already recovered its full investment in Orapa at the time of renegotiation. They argued that 25 to 33 percent of operating profits after the full return of principal was still a tidy yield. DeBeers, in fact, continued to expand its operations in Botswana by developing a new mine at Jwaneng. The claim that the govern-ment had not clearly defined a policy for future foreign investment and government participation, however, was justified.

The government seemed to fear that it had pushed its advantage in the DeBeers negotiations too far. It began to seek the opinions of foreign business leaders on economic policy initiatives under consideration in the government. If these consultations represent the start of a new policy toward the business community, the results should be highly bene-ficial to everyone.

As Table 5.1 indicates, Botswana's mineral output after a decade of independence was largely confined to coal, copper-nickel, and diamonds. A limited number of semi-precious stones was also produced for native craftsmen who fashion them into objets d'art and curios.

TABLE 5.1
MINERAL PRODUCTION, 1965-1977

Year	Manganese ore (tons)	Talc (tons)	Asbestos (tons)	Semi precious stones (kg)	Coal (tons)	Copper/ nickel matte (tons)	Diamonds, export value (Million R)
1965	7,873	-	806	-	-	-	-
1966	-	-	-	-	-	-	-
1967	1,114	76	-	-	-	-	-
1968	8,955	124	-	1,835	-	-	0.1
1969	24,520	51	-	6,044	-	-	0.2
1970	48,311	36	-	12,584	-	-	2.7
1971	35,603	160	-	104,612	-	-	5.3
1972	687	-	-	100,289	-	-	19.5
1973	340	-	-	72,914	-	-	23.2
1974	-	-	-	81,000	25,498	6,663	33.0
1975	-	-	-	65,000	68,639	16,513	31.7
1976-77	-	-	-	na	17,000	40,000	na

6. Manufacturing and Service Industries

Manufacturing is a fledgling activity in Botswana's economy. It accounted for only 5 percent of GDP in 1976/7 and was probably responsible for little more than 1 percent of capital formation. The largest enterprise is the Lobatse abattoir, which is operated by the Botswana Meat Commission (see Chapter 4). Otherwise there are few firms in Botswana, and they are small. Total employment in 1976 was approximately 2,500, or 6 percent of the labor force.

Growth of the sector is restricted by the size of the domestic market, the lack of skilled labor and infrastructure, and free trade within the Southern Africa Customs Union area. Botswana's production for the larger Customs area market is limited because electricity and water rates in Botswana are higher than in South Africa. The short-run outlook for rapid growth of manufacturing is not promising.

According to UN sources, there were fifty-five manufacturing firms, each with at least ten employees, in Botswana in 1973. Sixty-seven percent of these were wholly owned by foreigners; 25 percent were partly owned by foreigners. Batswana owned only 7 percent. Of the fifty-five, only twenty-eight (excluding the Botswana Meat Commission) were wholly operational. The sector's dependence on imports (excluding meat operations) was high. Import costs accounted for 33 percent of the gross value of sales. Value added in Botswana represented 44 percent of the value of sales.

The Customs Union agreement contains provisions that provide tariff protection within the Union for infant industries. Botswana invoked this provision to protect a brewery and soft drinks project that commenced production in 1976. The brewery's equity capital was provided by the BDC. The government was the majority shareholder and a German and a Swiss concern were minority stockholders. As a result of a stiff import tariff, the local beer was priced lower than imported beers. The impact of the tariff, however, caused the price of beer to rise considerably, especially in western Botswana, which is distant from the brewery.

Additional processing activity may be encouraged by Botswana's associate status within the European Economic Community. As long as goods exported to the EEC contain at least 50 percent value added by processing in an associated country, they can enter Europe duty-free. Botswana's government officials believe that this provision and their own accelerated capital depreciation and liberal profit repatriation policies for foreign investors offer considerable scope for profitable agriculture-based manufacturing and processing industries.

The service industries, especially commercial services, were stimulated by the advent of large mining operations in Botswana. Tables 2.2 and 2.3 showed the absolute and relative growth of the trade and financial sectors during the country's first decade. Wholesale and retail trade activity increased 1000 percent; financial services (banking, insurance, etc.) increased 1200 percent. This growth reflects the activities of the BDC, which sponsored and supplied partial financing for insurance, accounting, secretarial, maintenance, and repair services firms. It has encouraged the development of industrial and commercial parks near urban centers. Indeed, the first occupant of the Broadhurst industrial area, adjacent to Gaborone, was Prinz Bräu Botswana, the new brewery.

The Botswana Insurance Company was established in 1975 by the British insurance brokers, J. H. Minet and Company. They also provided the reinsurance and management services required to ensure that the new company had the necessary protection and expertise. In 1976, premium income from operations in Botswana rose to more than R3 million, a significant increase over the small amounts collected by itinerant agents from South African companies ten years earlier.

Until 1976, Botswana's monetary and financial system was an integral part of South Africa's. The South African rand was legal tender in Botswana, the country's international reserves were incorporated into South Africa's, and there was little formal regulation of Botswana's financial system. The Bank of Botswana Act and The Financial Institutions Act, passed in 1975, gave extensive regulatory powers to the newly established bank and to the Minister of Finance and Development Planning. A new currency, the pula (the name means "rain" or "beneficence" and was chosen by a popular poll), was put into circulation in late 1976. During its first few months, it was guaranteed to exchange at par with the rand. After a currency exchange, the accumulated rand were sent to South Africa in return for South African Reserve Bank balances. These balances became part of the initial foreign reserves of the Bank of Botswana. Government officials were surprised by the size of the cash balances that the population held, especially in the west.

The Bank of Botswana acts as banker and fiscal agent for the government. It is empowered to make temporary advances to the government and to buy and sell government securities. Two commercial banks, Standard Bank, Ltd., and Barclays, both subsidiaries of British banks, continue to operate in Botswana. Standard Bank, Ltd. served as the government's banker for the first ten years, although the government has recently placed deposits with Barclays as well.

Rapid economic growth in Botswana was accompanied by rapid growth in bank deposits and loans. Loans to businesses accounted for most of the growth in bank assets; time deposits, especially by the government, were the biggest liability during the period for which comprehensive banking data are available. (Table 6.1)

Because of the common currency, Botswana's residents could freely use South African banks; therefore, the data for Botswana's banks understate the financial operations of the Botswana economy. Although loans to the mineral development sector of the economy showed the most rapid increase, loans to the agriculture sector also multiplied because local banks were more willing to finance small-scale farmers. The government was a net creditor of the banks in Botswana and placed its surplus funds locally. Individual savings also increased in the country. As a result of these developments, the banking system developed considerable liquidity after 1973, which was placed abroad. Thus, the rudimentary banking system operated to produce an export of Botswana's internally generated savings.

The new currency and banking structure will give Botswana more control over its own monetary, fiscal, and exchange rate policies than it has ever had. The greater size and sophistication of the South African economy, however, will restrict the amount of independence it can actually achieve.

TABLE 6.1
CONSOLIDATED BANKING STATISTICS
(Barclays Bank, Standard Bank, National Development Bank, and Botswana Building
Society. Prior to 1976, figures exclude the National Development Bank.)

ASSETS

As at end of Period	Cash	Balances at Bank of Botswana	Balances due for other Banks	Treasury Bills	Loans and Advances	Investments	Other Assets	Total Assets
1972 Dec	0.9	-	22.4	-	14.3	1.1	2.9	41.6
1973 Dec	1.7	-	28.4	-	23.3	1.1	10.7	65.2
1974 Dec	2.1	-	37.3	-	39.8	1.2	24.2	104.4
1975 Dec	2.7	-	61.3	-	57.6	1.7	29.6	152.9
1976 Mar	1.7	-	30.3	-	75.2	1.8	9.2	118.2
Jun	2.3	-	33.5	-	70.6	1.8	10.3	118.4
Sep	3.9	10.4	10.7	-	72.3	1.8	22.8	121.9
Dec	3.7	18.7	2.1	8.6	76.4	1.8	7.5	118.8

LIABILITIES

As at end of Period	Balances due to other Banks	Government Deposits and Loans	Deposits from the Public			Capital & Reserves	Other Liabilities	Total Liabilities
			Current and Call	Savings	Fixed time and Shares			
1972 Dec	5.9	6.7	13.3	5.2	8.8		1.6	41.6
1973 Dec	3.6	12.5	16.6	7.3	12.5		12.7	65.2
1974 Dec	13.7	20.8	20.3	9.2	17.5		23.0	104.4
1975 Dec	29.6	42.4	21.2	11.0	18.3		30.4	152.9
1976 Mar	2.6	45.3	19.7	11.8	26.9	4.8	7.0	118.2
Jun	2.0	43.8	20.2	12.4	24.8	4.9	10.3	118.4
Sep	1.2	21.4	36.6	13.5	31.6	4.9	12.7	121.9
Dec	1.0	24.2	33.1	13.7	32.2	5.6	9.0	118.8

7. Foreign Trade and the Balance of Payments

Botswana's foreign trade is influenced not only by its geography and history, but also by its membership in the Southern Africa Customs Union, to which Lesotho, South Africa, and Swaziland also belong. This Customs Union agreement allows goods to move freely among the member countries. It requires members to apply the same import duties to goods entering their countries from outside the Customs Union. In practice, this has meant that South Africa's tariff schedules have been adopted by the smaller members and that their industries are subject to the same protective structure as South Africa's industries. The tariff of a less developed country usually protects local consumer goods industries but permits capital goods, machinery, and equipment to enter either without duty or at low duty rates. The South African tariff, however, has been highly protective across the industrial span. This protection has not helped local industry to flourish in the small member countries, because their economies are open to competition from South African industry, which is already equipped to serve a large-scale market.

Membership in the Customs Union is a mixed blessing. Botswana's share of the aggregate revenues collected by the

customs area is its most important source of income, providing
nearly two-thirds of its total tax revenues in recent years.
Botswana's share of the Custom Union's revenue pool (customs duties and excise and sales taxes) reflects the ratio of
Botswana's imports to the total value of imports by all members. Because revenue receipts lag two years behind the
determining trade flows, Botswana's receipts from the Customs Union through 1975/6 continued to show the large
imports associated with the construction at Selebi-Pikwe,
even though the copper-nickel project had been essentially
completed in 1974. The downturn in world economic activity
and higher oil prices of 1974 finally caused customs revenues
to drop sharply in 1976/7.

Such volatility led Botswana to undertake a renegotiation
of the customs-sharing formula in late 1976. It sought amend-
ments that would limit fluctuations. In the mid-1970s,
Botswana's customs revenues averaged 20 percent of the
value of imports. In 1976/7, the ratio fell to 17 percent.
Botswana finally succeeded in reaching an agreement that
prevented receipts from fluctuating below 17 percent or
above 23 percent of the value of imports.

Although no longer a part of the Rand Monetary Area,
Botswana has continued to use the same exchange controls it
established when it was required to align its monetary system
with the Customs Union. Requests for import permits have
to be filed in Botswana, but they are freely granted to all
petitioners. Goods from South Africa do not require import
licenses; goods from outside the Customs Area do require
licenses, which entitle the holder to buy the necessary foreign
exchange. In practice, therefore, there have been no import
controls. Export controls have not been used for exchange
control, but for revenue or as marketing devices (e.g., meat
and diamond exports). In addition, a 1956 customs agreement permits duty-free movement of goods between Botswana
and Rhodesia, provided they are not to be reexported. (This
excludes imports of Rhodesian beer, tobacco, and cigarettes.)

Membership in the Customs Union thus provides Botswana with a major source of income, especially during periods of rapid economic growth, when it is most needed. Open competition from South African industry forces industry in Botswana to be as efficient as South Africa's to survive. This probably means that only small businesses can compete. But because of the size and diversity of the South African market, Botswana's membership in the Customs Union is not likely to be the main constraint on Botswana's industrial growth in the foreseeable future. The lack of skilled labor and venture capital in Botswana, the high transport costs required to serve South African consumers, the quantitative import restrictions, and the general business recession in South Africa have slowed manufacturing growth in Botswana and limited exports to South Africa. Opportunities to produce for the large South African market are likely to be negligible as long as that country suffers high unemployment, declining investment, and rising defense expenditures.

The infant-industry exception to the Customs Union agreement (see Chapter 6) permits Botswana to protect its domestic market from South African competition, but only at the expense of high internal prices. The protective South African (and therefore Customs Union) tariff structure results in internal prices considerably above world market levels. (Duties collected average 11 percent of the c.i.f. value of imports at the South African border.) An additional duty applied by Botswana to the South African price plus internal freight charges would cause an even higher cost of living and doing business in Botswana.

It is estimated that about 75 percent of Botswana's imports come from South Africa. The rest come from other African countries and from Europe. Technical and security considerations limit data availability and precision. Data collection in Botswana is a new operation; the country's borders are long, and trained manpower is scarce. Consequently, a number of border crossings are unattended and trade is only partially recorded. In addition, trade with Rhodesia, which is permitted by a special dispensation from the UN-sponsored embargo, is unreported for security purposes. Before the UN embargo, Botswana imported primarily food products from Rhodesia and may still be doing so. Rhodesian procurement is forbidden by all aid-donor agencies, and only in the northern parts of Botswana are Rhodesian goods competitive.

During the early 1970s, imports expanded at an average annual rate of 34 percent, primarily because of the machinery and equipment required for the construction phase of the copper-nickel project at Selebi-Pikwe. In 1974, the rate of increase slowed markedly with the completion of that project (Table 7.1). The large jump in import value in 1975 was more a result of inflation and depreciation of the rand than of volume increase. (Data on the latter are not available.)

The country's dependence on imports has been described in earlier chapters. Botswana imports all the cooking oil, tea, sugar, and matches consumed in the country, as well as 50 percent of its grain requirements. It also imports all petroleum products, all capital equipment, and most materials and supplies for consumer goods production. Almost all of the imports enter through South Africa, and most of them are produced there. A closing of the South African border for any extended period of time would devastate Botswana's economy and cause widespread suffering among its people.

The structure of Botswana's exports has shifted with the change in its industrial structure. Mineral products replaced meat as the most important export in 1975 (Table 7.2). Together, they accounted for nearly 90 percent of mineral exports and copper-nickel for 40 percent in that year. The persistent growth of meat exports during the 1970s conceals Botswana's marketing problems during the years 1973–1975. These problems intensified in 1974, while Botswana was negotiating with the European Economic Community for continued access to EEC markets, especially to the United

TABLE 7.1
IMPORTS OF GOODS 1966-1975[a]
(R million)

Category	1966	1967	1968	1969/70[b]	1970/71[b]	1971/72[b]	1972	1973	1974	1975
Food and live animals	..	..	..	..	..	..	7.9	12.6	14.8	18.8
Beverages and tobacco	..	..	..	..	..	..	3.2	4.9	6.1	9.4
Crude materials, inedible, except fuel	..	..	..	..	..	..	1.	3.3	1.5	2.0
Mineral fuels, lubricants and related matter	..	..	..	..	..	..	3.9	5.1	13.4	15.2
Animal and vegetable oils and fats	..	..	..	..	..	..	0.2	0.1	0.3	0.5
Chemicals	..	..	..	..	..	..	2.9	6.2	6.1	6.9
Manufactured goods classified mainly by material	..	..	..	..	..	..	21.1	21.2	24.5	33.5
Machinery and transport equipment	..	..	..	..	..	..	33.6	44.4	33.8	38.6
Miscellaneous manufactured articles	..	..	..	..	..	..	8.5	9.3	14.0	18.6
Commodities and transactions n.e.c.	..	..	..	..	..	..	1.8	4.7	7.1	13.7
TOTAL	18.8	22.4	23.2	34.3	44.8[c]	60.8	84.0	111.7	121.5	157.2

[a] Commodity breakdown for earlier years not available.
[b] Financial years 1/4-31/3.
[c] After 1970/71 re-exports have been deducted from imports.

TABLE 7.2
EXPORTS OF GOODS, 1966-1975[a]
(R million)

Category	1966	1967	1968	1969/70[b]	1970/71[b]	1971/72[b]	1972	1973	1974	1975
Meat & meat products	..	..	..	..	..	..	18.6	30.7	32.7	36.4
Hides & skins	..	..	..	..	..	..	0.8	2.0	1.6	1.6
Other animal products	..	..	..	..	..	..	0.1	0.5	0.8	1.2
Mineral products	..	..	..	..	..	..	19.5	23.2	38.4	53.7
Other commodities	..	..	..	..	..	..	5.6	7.3	9.3	11.7
TOTAL	10.8	9.2	7.5	13.1	2.0	31.0	44.6	63.7	82.8	104.6

[a] Inclusive of re-exports.
[b] Financial years (1/4-31/3).

Kingdom (see Chapter 4). The reinstatement of Britain as Botswana's most important export market in 1975 was due to a temporary abatement of EEC import levies. The original six-month abatement was extended in additional six-month intervals through 1976. Late in that year, the EEC agreed to a twelve-month quota for 1977, with 60 percent of the quota to be exported during the first six months, which is the peak slaughter period.

Like most capital-importing developing countries, Botswana's balance of trade has been consistently negative. The trade deficit has varied with the rate of development. The small decline in the trade deficit in 1976 resulted from full production at, and increased exports from, Selebi-Pikwe.

Invisibles have added to the current account deficit (Table 7.3). The apparent surplus on freight account is the result of a convention in balance-of-payments accounting that separates the revenue earned by the Botswana section of Rhodesian Railways from the expenses incurred. This offsetting expense is entered under "Other Services" in Table 7.3. "Other Services" also includes the earnings of Batswana working in South African mines, which increased substantially in 1975 because of higher recruitment levels and increased wage rates. Payments of investment income to foreigners decreased during the 1970s as a consequence of the renegotiation of the DeBeers contract for diamond operations. In addition, there were losses, rather than expected gains, on the copper-nickel project in 1975 and 1976. Unless copper and nickel prices on world markets rise sharply, it will be some time before investment income payments by Selebi-Pikwe become substantial. The new diamond mine south of Orapa, however, will contribute to a resumption of the former upward trend. Travel has provided the only net credit among invisibles. Although this credit has remained small, both payments and receipts on travel account have been growing rapidly. Overall, the net deficit on invisibles has declined while the trade deficit has expanded in recent

TABLE 7.3
BOTSWANA: BALANCE-OF-PAYMENTS ESTIMATES, 1971-1975
(R million)

	1971	1972	1973	1974	1975
Exports, f.o.b.	27.4	44.3	63.7	74.3	92.7
Imports, c.i.f.	-55.6	-75.7	-94.7	-123.9	-160.3
Balance of trade	-28.2	-31.4	-31.0	-49.6	-67.6
International freight, in surance, and other transportation (net)	na	na	na	na	13.3
Investment income (net)	na	na	na	na	5.6
Travel (net)	na	na	na	na	2.0
Other services (net)	na	na	na	na	-13.6
Balance of goods and services	-34.8	-61.3	-61.7	-65.7	-60.3
Transfers (net)	5.4	8.5	14.3	7.8	9.4
Balance on current account	-29.4	-52.8	-47.4	-57.9	-50.9
Private nonmonetary long-term capital	na	na	na	na	27.1
Private nonmonetary short-term capital[a]	na	na	na	na	14.3
Government capital	na	na	na	na	34.5
Errors and Omissions	-1.0	2.2	9.0	-0.4	-13.9
Overall surplus (including allocation of SDRs)	7.2	18.9	14.3	8.2	11.1
"Monetary movements"[b]	-7.2	-18.9	-14.3	-8.2	-11.1

Source: U.S. Embassy and Central Statistics Office.

[a]Excludes estimated change in currency in circulation.
[b]Comprises changes in government balances held outside Botswana,
the commercial banks' net foreign position, and currency in
circulation.

years. The result is that the goods-and-services balance has remained roughly constant.

The Botswana government receives transfers of substantial amounts from two sources—grants from foreign governments and international agencies and payments from the operation of the Customs Union Agreement. Offsetting transfers by expatriates and other foreigners working in Botswana are also included in this category. (The money sent home by Batswana working in South African mines is treated as an income flow and included among invisibles.)

The large current account deficits in the 1970s are a

measure of the net inflow of capital. Because of the strength of Botswana's planning mechanism, the economic feasibility of its planning goals, and the vigor of its leadership, Botswana has been a favored applicant among aid donors. In contrast to the United States, which has provided only token amounts of aid resources to date, the international institutions and European governments (especially the Scandanavian countries and the United Kingdom) have consistently included Botswana among the list of countries to receive multilaterally and bilaterally extended credits and grants. During the years 1972–1975, Botswana received an average of $75 million from grants and credits on concessional terms and from private direct investment from the developed countries and international agencies* —a sizeable sum for a country of fewer than 700,000 people.

Botswana expects its international financial position to improve over the next few years. Officials predict that foreign exchange reserves will accumulate because of continuing capital inflows of both public and private funds. Private investment in diamond mining continues, and the Selebi-Pikwe operations, which reached capacity production levels late in 1976, are expected to reduce losses there. By mid-1977, Bank of Botswana reserves amounted to the equivalent of more than six months of imports. The new pula had appreciated 5 percent in value against the rand and the U.S. dollar. Strengthening of the international reserve position will give greater security to import maintenance in the face of fluctuations in foreign exchange income from such products as copper and nickel. (Diamonds, whose price and output are maintained by stockpiling when market demand is sluggish, are less sensitive to cyclical shifts.)

Until recently, Botswana's economy was fully integrated into the South African economy and monetary system.

*OECD, "Development Cooperation," *1976 Review* (Paris: November 1976).

International reserves did not become important until Botswana established its own currency unit, the pula. In the spring of 1977, these reserves amounted to P65 million. The currency in which they will be held—rand, sterling, dollars, or some other—and the size of the holdings will be determined by the new financial managers. The pula-rand exchange rate will be a key factor in these decisions.

Botswana's international payments position also depends on developments largely beyond its control. The prices of copper, nickel, and beef—the country's chief exports—are determined by world market conditions and are highly volatile. In addition, the price of beef is affected by the EEC's internal agricultural policy and its willingness to treat imports from Botswana as a special case. Net capital movements will depend on aid decisions made in other countries and on the climate for private investment, especially in the politically unstable south African countries. As operations at Selebi-Pikwe become more profitable, debt repayment will rise. Thus, the deficit in current account is likely to continue, and accumulation of reserves will depend on the climate for public and private investment.

8. Summary and Outlook

Botswana's natural endowments are a mixed blessing. Farming and ranching are limited by climatic and soil conditions, but mineral deposits may prove to be a source of considerable wealth. In several respects, initial returns from exploration and development justify moderate optimism. A landlocked country, however, suffers obvious economic and political disadvantages, which can only be counterbalanced by a skillfully fashioned public policy.

Major Vulnerabilities and Strengths

Botswana's disadvantages as a landlocked country are vastly intensified by the political turmoil in surrounding countries. It suffers higher transport costs because it has no direct access to the sea and no control over the cost of transit to the sea. Its access to the sea depends on the policies of the present white governments and their opponents, the black and white guerrilla and reform groups. Uncertain access to the outside world increases the risks of doing business in Botswana. Botswana's position is clearly vulnerable; nonetheless, it has several advantages.

When Botswana gained its independence, a traditional

tribal leader, who was diligent, devoted, and politically skill-ful, became head of state. The abilities and dedication of Sir Seretse Khama and his wife Ruth explain the political stability and the racial harmony in Botswana during the first ten years. By their interracial marriage years ago, Sir Seretse and his wife showed that they were far ahead of their times. Their enlightened attitude has benefited the people they later returned to lead.

The president and his family have set the tone and the standard, but emulation has been easy for the Batswana. Although classified by anthropologists as eight separate tribes, the Batswana have many common attributes. They share a tradition of friendship, hospitality, and mutual aid, as well as a common language. This tradition of tribal har-mony differentiates Botswana from much of the rest of black Africa and provides an enormous advantage.

Political and racial harmony, domestically and inter-nationally, were encouraged by the history of good relations between the Batswana and their colonial protector, Britain. The fact that Britain did not attempt colonization left the country free from a patrimony of bitterness and vindictive-ness toward its white neighbors. This has enabled Botswana to cope well with changing circumstances in Rhodesia and South Africa. For example, "localization" of the labor force—bringing more Batswana into positions of skill and responsibility in order to replace expatriates—remains a goal of development and a pressing political issue, but it will not cause the government to fall.

Botswana's geography and economic dependence have limited the scope of its foreign policy. But the Khama regime transformed weakness into a source of strength. Botswana used the enormous contrast between its economic weakness and the economic strength of South Africa (and, to a lesser extent, that of Rhodesia) as a defensive weapon. By not maintaining a military force for more than ten years, the country has openly acknowledged that it could not defend its borders against its neighbors. By offering sanctuary only to bona fide refugees and by not allowing guerrillas to establish bases on its soil, it has deprived its neighbors of any excuse for an invasion of its territory. Moreover, such an invasion would place the opprobrium of world opinion upon the invader. The Khama regime has comported itself with dignity and propriety in its relations with its neighbors, white and black, and has in no way compromised its principles of democracy and human rights by acknowledging the harsh reality of its dependence. Through its first decade, it has walked this foreign-policy tightrope with great success. There have been few border violations, and transport links with the outside have been maintained.

Skilled and devoted leadership and a history free of cultural or racial bitterness have endowed Botswana with advantages as difficult to exaggerate as they are to measure. The institutional foundations of Botswana's economy have provided an essential base for accomplishment; the economic development that has occurred would not have been possible without them. They were instrumental in attracting and retaining the services of highly motivated and qualified personnel for cabinet posts and for other high civil service positions, many of which are filled by European expatriates. These qualities were also responsible for attracting the public and private foreign capital that has provided the immediate basis for growth.

The domination of Botswana's economy by developments in South Africa has some compensating advantages. Those industries in Botswana that survive in open competition with their established South African counterparts will have a healthy start toward successful competition in the larger world arena. Also, the intimate relations between the two economies mean that Botswana is a known quantity to South African businessmen; investment there seems no more risky to them than domestic investment, and may be less so. As one South African businessman in Gaborone observed,

"We have lived with the racial problems for a long time. To us they are not as inhibiting as they would be to you."

Botswana's commendable record was not entirely the result of skilled leadership and political stability. It was also favored by luck. The county's first major economic development effort took place in a propitious environment. World markets in the early 1970s were expanding as all major industrial countries approached a peak of prosperity. The volume and price of Botswana's major exports, meat and minerals, increased because of the world boom, and the investment climate became increasingly favorable. The subsequent world recession and inflation also affected Botswana, but to a lesser degree than other export-dependent economies. The stability of the monopolistic diamond market and the benefit of special treatment in the protected EEC agricultural market insulated Botswana from the full effects of the depressed world market. Investment activity fell off, but export receipts continued to rise.

Botswana's economy is, therefore, not without impressive sources of strength. These strengths explain the miracle of its rapid economic growth, which surpassed all expectations. Will they sustain the economy enough to counteract its vulnerability?

The Outlook

Limited susceptibility to changes in world market conditions will continue as long as diamonds remain an important export and as long as the exemption from the EEC import levy prevails. Both circumstances seem likely to continue. DeBeers has firm plans to expand diamond mining output from the newly discovered richer diamond pipes. Botswana's meat exports are an insignificant fraction of total EEC supplies, but are vastly important to Botswana. Thus, any revocation of the exemption would appear to be an act of vindictiveness on Europe's part. The EEC remains apprehensive about the dangers of establishing precedents for exemptions, especially for its politically sensitive Common Agricultural Policy. Therefore, Botswana will probably have to continue to lobby for the exemption. Its retention, however, seems likely.

Botswana's favored position as a recipient of foreign aid from governments and international institutions also seems assured. Decisions to grant aid to Botswana have been soundly based on Botswana's carefully devised and articulated plans for development. Only if the character of its government changes markedly, which is unlikely, would the flow of foreign aid sharply decline.

The future of private foreign investment is less clear. The climate for investment worldwide, and especially in southern Africa, will be the important determinant. Even if there are no border violations by guerrilla groups, Botswana will remain vulnerable to interruptions in railroad services. These could occur in either Rhodesia or South Africa. A long interruption would disrupt the smooth flow of materials, supplies, and products, and increase transport costs. South Africa undoubtedly has the truck capacity to maintain the flow of Botswana's commodity trade moving across its border by rail. (Botswana's trade represents only an insignificant fraction of the total tonnage hauled by the South African transport net.) It is unclear, however, whether South Africa would be willing and able to do so during such a crisis.

Interruptions of rail service in Rhodesia are likely to be easier to cope with than those in South Africa. Interruptions lasting for a matter of days are nuisances. If there are many of them, they will add to cost, but if their duration is limited to the period covered by normal inventories, they will not cause serious hardship. For interruptions of longer duration, special alternative arrangements could be made if South Africa is willing and able to cooperate. If Botswana's border with Rhodesia closes for any extended period, South Africa's cooperation in providing rolling stock, additional trucking capacity, and perhaps skilled labor would be essential. The ultimate nightmare would be a closure of the South African border. Though it is unlikely that the entire border could be closed for very long, a major prolonged closure, perhaps accompanying a disruption of internal transport in South Africa, would cause great suffering in Botswana.

It is, of course, possible to construct a great number of political scenarios with different degrees of political disruption, bloodshed, and destruction in Botswana and in the adjacent areas. The economic consequences for Botswana would become progressively more devastating. Such speculation serves no purpose here except to remind us that it is always dangerous to project the past into the future. In Botswana's case, such dangers are especially acute.

But it is important not to exaggerate the problem. Botswana is fortunate to have an intelligent, resourceful population and a tradition of coping with natural disasters. During periods of drought, for example, people share available water. Such attitudes and customs help alleviate these burdens.

A British transport consultant to Botswana commented, "No other country in the world is faced with quite the same combination of transport disadvantages and advantages."* The concentration of 80 percent of the population along the railroad line in the east would ease distributional problems in an emergency. But without supplementary transport equipment and personnel, this advantage would be insignificant.

Botswana, then, is most vulnerable to political conditions in neighboring countries, which are beyond its control. Whether the full impact of this vulnerability ever strikes Botswana remains to be seen. Apart from this, the future is bright.

Given a reasonably favorable investment climate, the opportunity for further economic growth in Botswana

---

*J. F. R. Brown, "Republic of Botswana National Transport Plan State I," *Report to the Ministry of Overseas Development* (April 1976), p. 20.

clearly exists. The relatively rapid growth of air traffic between the populous eastern parts of Botswana and the western and northern sections of the country, *despite* a government policy not favorable to air transport development, is strong circumstantial evidence of growth potential in the outlying areas. In addition, the recent stress on rural development programs will benefit these sections. Rationalization of ranching practices, including higher slaughter rates, would increase the demand for better transport conditions between east and west. An upgrading of the road network would further encourage settlement and development of the west. Similarly, expanded food-crop acreage for the cash market would increase the demand for better roads, and better roads would encourage a wider dispersion of the population. An improved road link to the northwest was completed late in 1976. It will provide easier access to the Okavango delta area, where water is less of a problem, but where additional health hazards require special precautions.

The cash market for food within Botswana will grow if the urban areas and ranching operations continue to grow. The latter will depend on the level of investment within the country and the growth rate of incomes. In addition, a natural market for Botswana's food crops and beef exists in South Africa and Zambia, and to a lesser extent, in Angola and Mozambique. These markets are currently shut off by import controls that were introduced for balance-of-payments reasons. The political stability of its neighbors and the revival of their export industries—two enormous qualifications—would allow Botswana to carry on greater trade with its neighbors.

Rural development in Botswana—rationalization of ranching and expansion of cash-crop acreage—could also stimulate the growth of satellite industries that would produce agricultural raw materials for the European market. As an associate of the EEC, Botswana's manufactured exports qualify for preferential tariff treatment in the Common

Market, provided that at least 50 percent of the value of these exports is added locally. An expansion of the tiny local leather industry would take advantage of the special tariff treatment. This industry is thought to have great potential.

Within official circles in Botswana, speculative discussion about the future frequently turns to the possibility of a rail link to Walvis Bay, the port to the west in Namibia. An east-west rail link would supplement the existing north-south line and would afford an alternative means of access to the outside world. At present, however, no economic justification exists for such an additional transport link. The concept, nonetheless, is engaging in terms of economic potential.

Given a propitious economic environment (buoyant export markets, rising incomes and investment, and relaxed tensions in southern Africa), an east-west rail link through Botswana, connecting Walvis Bay in the west with Maputo in the east, could become economically feasible.

Although geological surveys of Botswana's mineral wealth are not yet complete, copper has already been discovered in the west, near the Namibian border. Coal deposits seem widely scattered; salt, sodium sulphate, and soda ash are plentiful in the central region, and gold has been mined in the past. In general, the prospects for further finds give reason for optimism. Known mineral deposits in the west and central portions have not been exploited, in part because of the lack of infrastructure and the expense of providing it. A certain amount of international trade already takes place across the border with Namibia, despite poor roads, because proximity makes it profitable. Economic development in Namibia would encourage the interchange.

Thus, mineral development in the western and central parts of Botswana would help to justify, and would be justified by, the proposed rail link. In addition, the prospect of attracting people to the land for rural development appears to be better in Botswana than in many less developed countries. The special role of cattle and ranching in the priorities of the Batswana means that the competing attractions of an urban existence are less compelling.

The decision to establish an army—after a decade in which an active foreign policy operated successfully in a threatening external environment—must have been extremely difficult. Even if Botswana could deploy one of the most skilled and best-equipped armies in the world, the odds would still weigh heavily against it because of the strength of neighboring groups. The Batswana have no militaristic tradition, and their borders are long and open. From the beginning, the country has been able to devote all of its scarce resources to constructive growth; any diversion from this goal could only be made under extreme circumstances.

The leadership of any country must protect the integrity of its borders. When violations become sufficiently frequent, the leadership must take steps to defend its territory—futile as these steps may be. If events in southern Africa lead to bloodshed and widespread destruction in Botswana and in neighboring countries, it would be a great tragedy.

9. Conclusions: The Lessons of Botswana

The economic history of the Republic of Botswana provides an almost classic example of how a developing country with determined and devoted leadership can help itself. When independence was gained, the generally accepted assessment of Botswana's prospects emphasized the apparent weaknesses and ignored some very basic strengths. These forecasts missed the mark entirely. Observers noted the lack of infrastructure and the problems of a landlocked country. Perhaps because it was then an unknown quantity, they gave no weight at all to leadership—to the dogged determination and devotion with which the new leaders intended to pursue their goals. Observers focused on the country's modest resources—its tiny and untrained population, its limited known mineral endowment, its arid climate. The leadership was untested, but it has made all the difference in the world.

A propitious world economic environment aided Botswana's economic development, but the new leaders took advantage of every opportunity. They urged everyone—potential investors, South African officials, Common Market officials, United Nations officials—to participate. They mobilized their own resources, they prepared their positions with care, and they coordinated their own efforts to ensure that they were all working for the same ends. If genius is defined in terms of diligence,* these men and women were certainly of genius calibre.

The lesson is clear. A "bootstrap" economic development program can succeed. Foreign aid, in the form of financial and technical resources from public and private sources, is readily available for projects and programs when they seem to be economically feasible and when the developing country is willing to contribute substantial amounts of its own limited resources. The cost of providing the extended road and rail network and the power and water supplies for the projects at Selebi-Pikwe and Orapa was high for Botswana. It was high because of the number of skilled personnel required to plan and implement the schemes and because of the amount of public credit committed to their financial support. The fact that the country was willing to commit its own scarce resources to the projects encouraged foreigners to do so.

It now appears that the copper-nickel mine will be an economically marginal operation for some time. Its costs have been vastly inflated by either poor technical planning or management. This is the country's misfortune, but it is not the government's fault. However, it does point out the pitfalls of development. Even carefully articulated plans can go awry in implementation and even diligence does not guarantee immediate success.

An important factor in the economic achievements of the first decade was Botswana's willingness to seek foreign expertise to supplement its own meager supply of trained professional and technical talent in staffing the ranks of the senior civil service. Equally important was the reception accorded them. They were made to feel welcome—so much so that many of the top expatriate civil servants have been in their jobs for most of a decade. This is evidence of a large

---

*When asked "What is genius?" Goethe is reported to have replied, "Genius—it is diligence, diligence, diligence."

degree of trust and mutual respect between the Batswana in cabinet-level positions and the (mostly European) expatriate civil servants. The trust would not exist if the cabinet members had any doubt about the loyalties of the expatriates or if the expatriates themselves felt at all harassed, socially or professionally, because of their race. This is not to deny the strength of the pressures for "localization" or the dissatisfaction over progress achieved so far. The pressures are strong. They are, however, managed in a mature, pragmatic manner in order to maximize economic growth.

Not every developing country is as fortunate as Botswana, which has escaped an inheritance of resentment toward citizens of a former colonial power. The practical advantages of suppressing such bitterness are clearly documented by the major role that talented European expatriates have played and are playing in Botswana's self-help exercise. The country could not have accomplished what it has without their skills. To have forced their own people into top-level policy positions before they were qualified would have meant plans less carefully developed, projects less completely studied, and proposals less thoroughly documented. The risks of failure would have been greatly enhanced. Botswana's experience illustrates that even with this expertise, the risks are substantial.

It is fashionable today (1977) to encourage self-help in the developing countries. Self-help, however, is an alternative or supplement to foreign help only if it is soundly based on feasible plans and well managed and directed. Self-help depends on talented and devoted leaders in the developing country. Without these qualities of leadership, foreign help will be wasted.

Appendix A. Statistical Tables

TABLE A.1

AREAS OF BOTSWANA IN SQUARE KILOMETRES

| District | Land Tenure | | | District |
	State	Tribal	Freehold	Total
Central	25,800	116,560+	5,370	147,730
Chobe	20,790	-	6	20,800
Ghanzi	105,480	1,040	11,390	117,910
Kgalagadi	100,450	-	6,490	106,940
Kgatleng	-	7,960	-	7,960
Kweneng	-	35,890	-	35,890
Ngamiland	17,640	91,490	-	109,130
Southern	470	27,970	30	28,470
North-East	-	-	5,120	5,120
South-East	-	660	1,120	1,780
TOTAL	270,630	281,570	29,530	581,730

TABLE A.2

SEASONAL NORMAL RAINFALL
(Millimeters)

Station	Longterm Seasonal Norm.
Francistown	458
Gaborone	514
Ghanzi	415
Kanye	522
Kasane	692
Lobatse	569
Mahalapye	461
Maun	476
Mochudi	496
Molepolole	506
Palapye	304
Serowe	495
Shakawe	574
Tsabong	251
Tshane	338
Werda	-

TABLE A.3

FORMAL SECTOR EMPLOYMENT BY SECTOR, 1972-1975[a]

Sector	1972	1973	1974	1975
Freehold agriculture	5,058	5,092	5,108	5,262
Mining and quarrying	1,680	3,010	4,140	4,270
Manufacturing	2,302	2,310	2,491	2,600
Electricity and water	337	337	531	674
Construction	6,468	7,787	6,787	6,389
Trade, hotels, restaurants	6,046	6,874	7,029	7,300
Transport and communications	1,122	1,155	1,355	1,494
Finance, insurance, real estate and business services	975	1,134	1,155	1,230
Community and personal services	2,730	3,125	3,088	3,240
Education	2,731	3,350	3,808	4,415
Local Government	1,393	1,755	1,702	2,136
Central Government	9,328	10,371	12,219	13,047
Domestic servants	8,029	9,254	9,877	10,405
TOTAL	48,199	55,554	59,290	62,462
of which Noncitizens	3,708	3,940	3,962	4,027
Noncitizens, percentage of formal sector employment	8	7	7	6

[a]The sector breakdown is not quite comparable to
national accounts. 1972 employment figures as of
April/May, the other as of mid-August.

TABLE A.4

NUMBER OF PERSONS EMPLOYED BY CITIZENSHIP AND BY SEX, 1975

Sector	Citizens, Total	Noncitizens, Total	All Persons Males	Females	Total
Agriculture	3,145	40	2,722	463	3,185
Mining and quarrying	3,434	546	3,753	227	3,980
Manufacturing	3,218	135	2,840	513	3,353
Electricity and Water	516	93	639	15	654
Construction	7,106	454	7,360	200	7,560
Commerce	6,312	319	4,822	1,809	6,631
Transport and Communications	1,503	211	1,660	54	1,714
Finance	1,783	219	1,642	360	2,002
Community and Social Services	2,496	236	2,194	538	2,732
Education	3,671	710	1,751	2,630	4,381
Sub-Total	33,229	2,963	29,383	6,809	36,192
Central Government	5,733	500	4,951	1,282	6,233
Local Government	2,635	48	2,180	503	2,683
TOTAL	41,597	3,511	36,514	8,594	45,108
Central Government Industrial Class Employees	6,317	-	5,062	1,255	6,317

TABLE A.5

NUMBER OF PERSONS EMPLOYED BY LEVEL OF SKILL, 1975

Sector	ALL PERSONS								
	Professional & Technical Workers	Administrative and Managers	Skilled Office Workers	Skilled Sales Workers	Skilled Service Workers	Skilled Agriculture Workers	Skilled Production and Transport Workers	Unskilled Workers	Total
Agriculture	3	9	11	86	-	87	65	2,924	3,185
Mining and quarry	253	37	262	8	109	2	789	2,520	3,980
Manufacturing	69	55	159	29	19	19	539	2,464	3,353
Electricity and water	40	16	70	-	-	-	222	306	654
Construction	176	47	169	7	3	16	2,278	4,864	7,560
Commerce	111	118	305	1,376	200	22	445	4,054	6,631
Transport & communications	53	16	136	14	62	-	127	1,306	1,714
Finance	171	90	334	130	1	3	91	1,182	2,002
Community & social services	235	55	414	105	75	33	396	1,419	2,732
Education	4,103	7	56	5	15	-	9	166	4,381
Sub-Total	5,214	450	1,916	1,760	484	182	4,883	21,225	36,192
Central Government	1,585	126	2,491	5	1,752	87	187	-	6,233
Local Government	237	57	593	-	-	2	263	1,531	2,683
Total	7,036	633	5,000	1,765	2,236	271	5,333	22,756	45,108
Central Government Industrial Class Employees	-	-	280	-	145	121	2,064	3,707	6,317

TABLE A.6

NUMBER OF PERSONS EMPLOYED, BY LOCATION AND BY ECONOMIC SECTOR, 1975

Sector	LOCATION					
	Gaborone	Francistown	Lobatse	Selebi-Pikwe	Other Districts	Total
Agriculture	217	411	307	-	2,250	3,185
Mining and quarrying	72	-	79	-	1,120	3,980
Manufacturing	569	652	1,678	-	412	3,353
Electricity and water	654	-	-	-	-	654
Construction	4,780	691	127	1,336	626	7,560
Commerce	1,428	1,337	450	125	3,291	6,631
Transport and communications	1,346	282	36	-	50	1,714
Finance	1,550	68	51	146	187	2,002
Community and social services	598	506	25	230	1,373	2,732
Education	479	160	186	59	3,497	4,381
Sub-Total	11,693	4,107	2,939	4,647	12,806	36,192
Central Government	3,810	497	376	93	1,457	6,233
Local Government	409	325	144	230	1,575	2,683
Total	15,912	4,929	3,459	4,970	15,838	45,108
Central Government Industrial Class Employees	2,295	678	618	193	2,533	6,317

TABLE A.7

RECRUITMENT OF BATSWANA FOR SOUTH AFRICAN MINES
1970-1976

Year	Numbers Recruited				Deferred Pay (R'000)	Remittances (R'000)
	Total	Gold Mines	Platinum Mines	Other		
1970	35,921					
1971	31,592					
1972	23,678					
1973	28,955	21,088	3,967	3,900	2,785	
1974	27,405	18,000	5,508	3,897	3,738	
1975	34,020[a]	26,183	3,170	4,667	6,287	1,129
1976	39,214[a]	28,960	5,420	4,734	10,064	1,835

[a]Partly estimated.

TABLE A.8

GOVERNMENT REVENUE AND EXPENDITURE, 1949/50-1975/6

Year	Revenue R Million		Expenditure R Million	
	Recurrent	Development	Recurrent	Development
1949/50	1.4		1.4	
1955/6	1.9		2.2	
1959/60	3.8		4.4	
1964/5	8.3		11.9	
1965/6	11.0		15.1	
1966/7	11.6		17.8	
1967/8	15.0	4.4	15.7	3.8
1968/9	15.3	3.5	15.0	3.3
1969/70	17.4	5.1	14.0	4.9
1970/1	12.9	9.3	15.8	8.5
1971/2	19.9	12.1	19.4	12.3
1972/3	28.6	28.7	28.6	29.9
1973/4	42.4	28.6	40.9	30.3
1974/5	63.3	31.7	62.6	32.8
1975/6	79.5	37.3	72.3	35.4

TABLE A.9

GOVERNMENT REVENUE BY SOURCE 1972/3-1975/6

(R'000)

Source of Revenue	1972/3	1973/4	1974/5	1975/6
Customs and Excise (including sales duty)	12,469	20,941	30,398	24,606
Taxes and Duties	5,857	8,906	16,396	23,641
Licenses	649	684	914	1,041
Receipts in respect of Departmental Services	1,087	1,345	2,110	2,501
Posts and Telegraphs	1,684	2,041	- [a]	2a
Revenue from Government Property	3,951	4,613	4,449	15,691
Fines	92	112	135	209
Reimbursements	593	832	1,492	2,464
Loan Repayments	1,156	1,136	4,838	5,739
Interest	372	881	1,838	2,498
Miscellaneous	208	296	347	898
Total Ordinary Revenue	28,118	41,787	62,917	79,290
Total Grants and Loans	28,957	26,346	18,077	24,960
Total All Revenue	57,075	68,133	80,994	104,249

[a] Incorporated in Post & Telecommunications commercial account.

TABLE A.10
GOVERNMENT EXPENDITURE BY HEAD 1972/73-1975/6
AND ESTIMATES FOR 1976/7

(R'000)

Head	1972/3	1973/4	1974/5	1975/6	1976/7
Ordinary Recurrent Expenditure					
Parliament	87	100	300	171	179
Office of the President	2,620	3,315	4,677	6,386	7,090
Ministry of Finance and Development Planning	5,677	6,650	2,630	2,753	3,096
Ministry of Health, Labour and Home Affairs	2,104	2,515	2,366	1,401	1,634
Ministry of Agriculture	2,635	3,068	4,612	5,674	5,765
Ministry of Education	2,046	2,494	3,898	5,174	10,563
Ministry of Commerce and Industry	2,055	707	1,118	1,382	1,514
Ministry of Local Government and Lands	1,628	2,536	4,736	6,771	4,206
Ministry of Works and Communications	3,838	4,779	4,677	4,774	8,765
Ministry of Mineral Resources and Water Affairs	-	1,773	2,006	2,767	2,788
Ministry of Health[a]	-	-	1,823	4,001	4,395
Administration of Justice	88	106	142	208	229
Attorney General	1,033	1,139	1,558	1,814	2,095
Auditor General	62	71	92	102	134
Appropriations from Revenue	-	9,624	24,109	22,871	7,443
Public Debt	3,737	1,154	2,742	4,420	6,630
Pensions, Gratuities and Compensations	650	595	756	949	1,159
Salaries and Allowances - Specified Offices	27	31	38	39	43

Overseas Services and Scheme	287	276	276	350	260
Miscellaneous	20	1	-	327	40
Total Recurrent Expenditure	25,594	40,934	62,576	72,334	68,028
Expenditure from the Development Fund					
Ministry of Agriculture	594	517	1,711	1,262	2,439
Ministry of Commerce and Industry	1,011	266	437	430	1,601
Ministry of Mineral Resources and Water Affairs	-	1,112	2,810	3,550	4,554
Ministry of Finance and Development Planning	23,670	16,430	4,970	3,577	3,198
Ministry of Education	1,011	1,697	2,533	3,662	4,210
Ministry of Health, Labour and Home Affairs	347	217	170	254	252
Ministry of Local Government and Lands	840	4,131	8,879	10,560	6,104
Ministry of Works and Communications	2,282	5,812	16,625	11,274	31,047
Ministry of Health	-	-	425	482	1,740
Office of the President	128	85	275	398	1,191
Total Development Expenditure	29,883	30,267	32,785	35,449	56,336

[a] Ministry of Health became an independent Ministry in November 1974.

Appendix B. Government Policy
Toward Investment

1. Government Policy Toward Business Investment

The Botswana Government welcomes private business investment, both local and foreign, which provides employment and training for local citizens, reduces Botswana's reliance on imported products, upgrades local raw materials, generates further business opportunities, or otherwise diversifies the economy.

The Government requires public participation in the ownership and direction of major enterprises which have strategic economic importance for the country, and also of businesses which depend for their viability on the enjoyment of an official monopoly, preference, protected status or concession. A scheduled airline and a manufacturer who has been granted protection against competing imports are examples of such enterprises. The intention of this policy is to safeguard the country's interests and to assist private investors in a spirit of participation. Public participation is generally achieved by the Botswana Development Corporation taking a shareholding in businesses of these kinds and appointing representatives to their Boards.

Reprinted from "Business Investment in Botswana: A Brief Guide," published by the Botswana Development Corporation, Limited.

Manufacturing enterprises of significant size are required to obtain a manufacturing licence from the Ministry of Commerce and Industry, Private Bag 4, Gaborone, before beginning operations. The Ministry is prepared, if it is in the country's interests, to make a licence to manufacture specific products in Botswana exclusive to a particular company for a period of up to four years.

The Government is willing, in approved cases, to apply protective tariffs on imported goods which compete with the products of a newly-established local business. Such tariffs apply to imports from all countries, including Botswana's partners in the Southern Africa Customs Area, and are applied for a period of up to eight years. They may be extended beyond eight years with the consent of South Africa, Lesotho, Swaziland, and Namibia.

Expatriate employees are required to obtain residence permits and (except in the case of company directors) work permits from the Ministry of Health, Labour and Home Affairs, Private Bag 2, Gaborone. Where the expatriate possesses skills which are unobtainable among local citizens these permits are freely available, subject to a security check on the individual concerned. The Government requires local citizens to be trained to fill all posts as rapidly as reasonably possible.

Dividends, interest, technical fees, and royalty payments are freely remittable abroad, subject to the payment of withholding tax on dividends and interest.

Botswana is a signatory of the International Convention on the Settlement of Investment Disputes, which provides for independent international arbitration at the request of investors (or of the Government). An investment guarantee agreement is in force with the United States of America, and stringent safeguards against expropriation are contained in the Botswana Constitution.

2. Investment Guide to Botswana

1. Although the market for consumer goods in Botswana is very small, Botswana's membership in the Southern African Customs Union gives manufacturers in Botswana completely free and duty free access to the whole of the Southern African Customs Union Area market.

The size of this market is not known but the combined imports into the area are the equivalent of over U.S. $3,000 million (U.S. $3 billion). This indicates the size of the market which is not yet satisfield by local production either in South Africa or in any of the other countries in the Customs Union Area.

2. At the same time, goods manufactured in Botswana have access to African countries north of the Zambesi. Most of these markets prohibit imports of goods manufactured in South Africa.

3. Botswana is particularly interested in the following categories of industry:

a) Nationally strategic industries.
b) Basic or economically strategic industries.
c) Labour development industries.
d) Rural based industries.
e) Batswana owned industries.

Reprinted from "Investment Guide to Botswana," published by the Ministry of Commerce and Industry, Botswana.

4. Nationally strategic industries are those industries which will produce goods which make the country less dependent upon outside suppliers or which help to bring about a substantial diversification of Botswana's export trade. An example of such an industry is Botswana Oxygen Company, now being set up to manufacture industrial and medical gases.

5. Basic or economically strategic industries are those which produce materials or undertake services which make the establishment of other industries feasible. Examples include a large-scale tannery, a paper-making industry, a scrap metal rerolling mill, etc.

6. Labour development industries are those industries which not only provide a large number of employment opportunities for citizens but also provide ample opportunities for in-service training and the upgrading of citizen workers from unskilled labourers to fully skilled operatives and managers. Examples may include radio assembly or assembly of office machines (typewriters) or domestic equipment where initial activities are wholly simple assembly work with the upgrading of employees to undertake partial manufacture and, later, entire manufacture.

7. Rural based industries are those industries which are logically suited for establishment in a non-urban area because of the presence in a particular rural area of special raw materials or skills or because of climatic needs or problems concerning disposal of effluents, etc.

8. The following are possible areas for industrial investment:

A. LEATHER

a) Tannery to be situated at Lobatse—approximately 200,000 cattle hides and 15,000 goat skins available at BMC annually. Also possibility of additional quantities of hides and skins from other areas, being available for tanning.

b) When tannery is operative there should be excellent prospects for leather goods industries including:

    i. footwear;

   ii. sports goods;

  iii. industrial leather;

  iv. travel goods.

B. CLAY PRODUCTS AND CERAMICS, ETC.

a) Ample supplies of clays and non-metal minerals exist and some of these deposits are in close proximity to the coal mines, so that there should be no undue problems regarding fuel for clay products and ceramics production.

b) Clays have not been fully assayed for quality (a UN mission has been requested for this purpose). Related materials include gypsum, limestone, refractory clays.

c) Possible industrial investment opportunities include:

    i. Cement production—all cement at present imported but present demand now reaching 100,000 tons per annum and a cement factory becomes feasible—all the necessary materials are available;

   ii. Plaster of Paris;

  iii. Gypsum building board;

  iv. Domestic china, pottery and earthernware;

   v. Soil and irrigation pipes;

  vi. Bricks and tiles;

 vii. Refractories;

viii. Insulators;

  ix. Wall claddings;

   x. Terrazzo floorings and mosaics (from marble available at Kanye).

C. CHEMICALS, FINE CHEMICALS, AND DRUGS

a) Enzyme and hormone production from glands and offals at BMC.

b) Botanical extracts. The botanical resources of Botswana have never been commercially examined or exploited. Possibilities include:

i. Maytansine from Maytenus heterophylla and Maytenus senegulensis both of which plants grow
   extensively in Botswana (Maytansine is known to
   have anti-tumour activity);
ii. Water soluble gums including gum arabic;
iii. Essential Oils. There are a number of indigenous
    materials with pungent odours which have not
    been identified. Climatically Botswana is well
    suited for the cultivation of certain essential oil
    bearing plants;
iv. Wattle extracts.

c) Sodium chemicals and phosphates from the Sua Pan
   brine.
d) Coal chemicals.

D. PAPER, ETC.

Possibilities of the production of paper or paper-boards,
etc., from the Okavango papyrus.

E. MISCELLANEOUS MANUFACTURES

a) Industrial abrasives using Botswana's resources of
   agates and other semi-precious gemstones.
b) Diamond drilling equipment for minerals and water
   exploration.
c) Glass container factory (for brewery and soft drinks).
d) Electroplating.
e) Packaging industry (cartons, paperboard containers,
   milk and chibuku containers, etc.).
f) All forms of assembly industries—radios, domestic
   and office equipment, etc., making use of the manpower availability in Botswana and the access to markets both South and North of Botswana.

BOTSWANA ORIGIN

9. *a*) Goods can be described as "Made in Botswana"
   provided that:

    i. 25% of the costs of production occur in Botswana; and

    ii. the final production process occurs in Botswana.

For the purposes of calculating costs occurring in Botswana the following costs can be taken into account:

    i. Salaries and wages paid in Botswana (including salaries and wages paid to expatriates employed in Botswana as well as salaries and wages paid to Botswana citizens);

    ii. Rents for factory premises, electricity, heating, water, etc., provided these are used directly for production;

    iii. Immediate packages in which the goods are sold (bottles, cans, cartons, etc.,) but not costs of packing for carriage and transport;

    iv. Depreciation of manufacturing equipment and machinery;

    v. Materials of Botswana origin used in production;

    vi. All other costs including administrative costs which are directly related to the production of the goods. Costs for general administration and sales costs are not allowable;

b) The benefits of having the goods marked "Made in Botswana" are:

    i. Goods have free access to other countries of the Southern African Customs Union;

    ii. Goods have easy access to other African countries north of the Zambesi;

    iii. Goods have special preferential rates of duty in the U.K. and certain other Commonwealth countries;

    iv. Goods have special duty free and low duty preferences in countries such as Switzerland and Canada which have special measures to facilitate imports from the least developed countries.

TAX INCENTIVES IN BOTSWANA

10. *a*) The rate of Income Tax (Company) is 30%; and 10% to 15% ($900 to $38,400) resident personal tax. A flat 20% for nonresidents.

   b) The Income Tax Act provides the following investment allowances:

   i. 15% of the cost of an industrial building or improvements to any industrial building, in the year in which the building was first used or when the improvements were completed;

   ii. 25% of the expenditure on any plant and machinery in the first year in which it is used.

   c) The Income Tax Act also provides for the following annual allowances:

   i. 10% of the cost of industrial buildings or building improvements during the year in which the building was first used or in which the improvements were completed, and for the following nine years;

   ii. an allowance for expenditure on plant and machinery at whatever rate per annum the investor chooses provided that when the investor has claimed deductions totalling 100% of the expenditure he cannot make any further claim.

   d) Training allowance at 125% of the cost of all approved training activities (including the salary of a training officer).

   e) An allowance of R1,000 in respect to every house built for the purpose of accommodating employees.

   f) Development Approval Order. Development Approval Orders grant special allowances including complete tax holidays and financial incentive payments for industries of special interest to Botswana and particularly those falling within the categories mentioned in paragraph 3.

PROTECTION FOR INDUSTRIES

11. *a)* All industries which employ 10 or more persons or use 25 h.p. or more have to be licenced under the Industrial Development Act. An industrial licence is renewable annually and is renewed automatically unless there has been some very serious offence. An industrial licence costs R50 (approximately U.S. $62.50) per annum.

   b) All applications for industrial licences have to be advertised two weeks running in the Gazette and the Daily News. Any industrial licence holder can object to the granting of a licence to another project if he thinks that the competition will seriously affect his own business. Minister for Commerce and Industry will ask the Industrial Development Advisory Board to advise him where an objection has been lodged.

   c) In special cases, where there is need for a heavy investment or the industry needs to undertake extensive training or there are other unusual circumstances, an exclusive licence may be granted which prohibits the establishment of any competing industry in Botswana. Exclusive licences of this kind may be granted for a maximum period of four years in the first instance but in special circumstances the exclusivity may be extended for an additional four years.

   d) In order to protect infant industries which are established in Botswana from excessive competition, the Customs Union agreement permits Botswana to raise a special tariff on all imports of a particular type of product. This includes imports of goods manufactured in South Africa or any of the other countries in the Customs Union. There is no limit to the extent of duty which can be imposed. However, this is a "one way" protective measure. South Africa cannot impose duties against goods made in Botswana.

e) In the case of an industry which is established in Botswana and which has the capacity to supply virtually
the whole of the needs of the Customs Union area,
the industry can be "specified." Special duties against
and imports into the whole of the Customs Union
area can be arranged to provide such an industry with
protection against imports from overseas.

3. Assistance from the Botswana Development Corporation

The Botswana Development Corporation (BDC) is a limited liability company wholly owned by the Botswana Government. Established in 1970, its total net assets as of mid-1974 are approximately R6 ($9 million). Its investment programme for the period 1974–76 totals R5 million ($7.5 million). BDC's portfolio includes subsidiary companies involved in air services, property development, farming, engineering and construction, leasing, car rental, diamond valuing, beer and soft drinks manufacture and the operation of industrial estates. Associated companies are involved in hotel operations, insurance, estate agency, aircraft servicing, tyre retreading, weaving and secretarial services.

BDC is the main agency for financing commercial and industrial development in Botswana. It is concerned with businesses of practically all sizes although in practice it has not become involved in the establishment of small shops, workshops and farms, for which other financing agencies exist. It identifies and researches opportunities for profitable

Reprinted from "Business Investment in Botswana: A Brief Guide," published by the Botswana Development Corporation, Limited.

business investment in all sectors of the country's economy, and assists their implementation.

BDC is willing to assist in the preparation of market surveys and financial feasibility studies for any projected businesses. It also assists businessmen in negotiations with Government departments and in compliance with Government policy requirements.

BDC provides finance for many of the enterprises which are established in the country. This is negotiated individually to reflect the financial requirements and other circumstances of each case. BDC takes equity holdings, arranges options to purchase equity holdings, makes loans, and provides industrial sites, factory buildings, machinery and vehicles on lease. It also provides managerial assistance, where required, to affiliated companies. Strategic industries and enterprises which are dependent on Government concessions are generally required to have a shareholding held by BDC.

BDC provides financial assistance at commercial rates. However, it is prepared to make sub-commercial investments in the case of projects which offer outstanding economic or social benefits. It requires adequate security where it makes loans or lease arrangements, and detailed feasibility studies where it purchases shareholdings. In all cases information concerning the investors involved is required, including bankers' and auditors' references.

In general, BDC assists both local and foreign investors to establish viable businesses in Botswana by providing information, advice and capital.

4. Investment Policy

The Botswana Development Corporation's objectives are:

1. to create and/or
2. to promote, in Botswana, commercially viable businesses which either *i.* because of the nature of their products or services, or *ii.* because of the manner in which they are operated, will contribute to national goals as stated in the National Development Plan.

The National Development Plan favours the establishment of enterprises which will have potential for:

1. Generating significant employment;
2. Adding to the skills of Botswana nationals;
3. Producing products which can be substituted for imports;
4. Generating additional business opportunities;
5. Creating local entrepreneurs;
6. Contributing to the rural economy;
7. Upgrading natural resources;
8. Creating new national assets;

Reprinted from "General Information," published by the Botswana Development Corporation, Limited.

9. Diversifying the base of the economy; and
10. Contributing to the creation of a nationally owned commercial and industrial sector.

Applicants for assistance from the Botswana Development Corporation will be asked to demonstrate how their project will contribute in each of the above enumerated areas, and will specifically be called upon to present plans for training Botswana nationals to occupy, in due course, posts at all levels in the proposed enterprise.

The Botswana Development Corporation will participate as an investor in an enterprise when:

1. Either its financial and managerial assistance is necessary for the enterprise to be viable;
2. The Botswana Development Corporation's active presence at a policy making level will constructively influence the enterprise with respect to national goals; or
3. When an investment is likely to generate additional resources for reinvestment by the Corporation in accordance with its business objectives.

When investing its funds the Botswana Development Corporation will seek to:

1. Secure its principal;
2. Structure its investment in such a way that the financial strength of each assisted enterprise is increased; and
3. Arrange the terms of its investment so that when each assisted enterprise is successful, the Botswana Development Corporation will have the opportunity to realise a capital profit.

To secure its principal, the Botswana Development Corporation will not except in extraordinary circumstances:

1. Invest more than 15% of its net worth in any one project;
2. Invest more funds in any one project than the total of funds invested by the other ordinary shareholders;
3. Invest any funds in any project prior to signing agreements which will provide the Botswana Development Corporation with the ability to take remedial action should the value of its investment become endangered; and
4. Invest any funds in any project prior to the completion of a thorough feasibility study.

Applicants for assistance from the Botswana Development Corporation will be asked to cooperate with, and assist in, the preparation of a feasibility study, the undertaking of which will follow the satisfactory completion of a preliminary questionnaire.

To increase the financial strength of each enterprise which it assists, the Botswana Development Corporation will endeavor, as much as practicable, and within the limits imposed by its need to secure its principal, to provide equity capital in the form of convertible preference shares or near equity capital in the form of convertible loan stock, so that the borrowing capacity of each assisted enterprise is enhanced.

To arrange the terms of its investment so that when each assisted enterprise is successful, the Botswana Development Corporation will have the opportunity to realise a capital profit, the Botswana Development Corporation will ask the other shareholders in each assisted enterprise to waive their rights of first refusal should the Botswana Development Corporation desire to sell all or part of its position. When disposing of an investment the Botswana Development Corporation will firstly seek Botswana nationals as buyers.

5. Feasibility Study Requirements

NOTE: Enterprises seeking assistance from the Botswana Development Corporation will be asked to submit an analysis of the feasibility of their proposed business activity. Staff of the Botswana Development Corporation are prepared to assist applicants with the preparation of this analysis.

The following information is required in order for the Botswana Development Corporation to provide assistance. Further information than that asked for in this Memorandum may be needed:

1. A brief overview of the project including the economic rationale behind it.
2. A description of the potential sources of funds for the project and the terms upon which they will become available.
3. A list of licences, patents or permits required for the project.
4. A description of the markets for the products or services to be offered. This description must include both the type of market and its location.

Reprinted from "General Information," published by the Botswana Development Corporation.

5. A list of potential customers, competitors, actual and potential, and substitute products or services.
6. An analysis of the competitive edge that proposed products or services will have over the ones that are presently in the market place, or may be introduced to the market place.
7. An estimate of the gross sales of the proposed enterprise for the first five years of its business life, based upon the facts presented in numbers 4, 5, and 6 above.
8. A description of the production techniques to be employed and the reasons for using them.
9. Detailed studies of:
   a) the availability and cost of raw materials
   b) the availability and cost of water
   c) the availability and cost of power.
10. A plot plan showing the location and dimensions of land required and a discussion of the economic rationale for the location with particular reference to:
    a) proximity to the market place
    b) proximity to raw materials
    c) proximity to transport facilities
    d) proximity to the labour supply.
11. Descriptions, including architectural drawings if available, of all buildings required, plus details of the estimated costs of construction.
12. A complete list of equipment needed during the next five years, including quotations from suppliers for all equipment needed during the next twelve months.
13. A capital expenditure plan for the next five years.
14. A description of the managerial structure of the enterprise including an organisation chart.
15. A list showing the number and the potential sources of skilled workers to be employed, skills required, and the proposed wage rates.
16. A list showing the number of unskilled workers to be

employed, a general description of their jobs and the proposed wage rates.

17. A timetable covering the startup phase of the proposed enterprise, which will include the dates, and amounts of money involved in:
    a) the purchase of land
    b) the purchase of a building or buildings
    c) the purchase of machinery
    d) the employment of personnel
    e) the commencement of production
    f) the commencement of sales.

18. A projected profit and loss statement for a five year period.

19. An estimate of the enterprise's capitalisation based upon the data contained in 17 and 18.

20. A determination of the rate of return on total capital employed and on equity.

21. A description of how and if the proposed enterprise will contribute to:
    a) generating significant employment in Botswana
    b) adding to the skills of Botswana nationals
    c) producing products which can be substituted for imports
    d) generating additional business opportunities
    e) creating local entrepreneurs
    f) contributing to the rural economy
    g) upgrading natural resources
    h) creating new national assets
    i) diversifying the base of the economy
    j) contributing to the creation of a nationally owned commercial and industrial sector.

22. A plan for recruiting and training unskilled, skilled, and managerial personnel over the next five years to occupy posts at all levels in the enterprise.

6. The Government's Industrial Policy

General

The Government of Botswana is anxious to encourage the development of the commercial and industrial sectors of the economy. However it is not prepared to enter into self-defeating competition with surrounding countries as far as the incentives it is prepared to offer is concerned. Rather it aims to tailor its incentive package to meet the particular needs and aspirations of Botswana.

The highest priority is given to the creation of new job opportunities and it is considered that the expansion of manufacturing and processing industries should contribute significantly to the achievement of this objective.

The Government recognizes that significant industrial and commercial development will be achieved only if Botswana attracts substantial private investment and skilled manpower from abroad. The Government favours local participation in all ventures, either through private individuals or organisations or through the Botswana Development Corporation.

Reprinted from "General Information," published by the Botswana Development Corporation, Limited.

Botswana is a signatory of the International Convention on the Settlement of Investment Disputes and thereby has agreed to abide by all the rules of the International Centre for Settlement of Investment Disputes.

With particular regard to foreign investors the Constitution of Botswana, in subsection 2, declares that "no person . . . shall be prevented from remitting . . . the whole of that amount (compensation) . . . to any country of his choice outside of Botswana."

Botswana has entered an investment guarantee agreement with the United States of America and is currently negotiating a similar agreement with the Federal Republic of Germany.

Investment Incentives

Serviced Land

The Government intends to service 60 hectares of industrial land in Gaborone, 30 hectares in Francistown, 24 hectares in Selebi-Pikwe, and 20 hectares in Lobatse for industrial use over the next five years.

Tax Incentives—General

The Income Tax Act 1973 provides for reliefs on capital expenditure that are more attractive than many tax holiday arrangements found elsewhere.

The cost of plant and machinery may be written off as and when the business wishes whilst new factory, manufacturing and hotel plant qualifies for a 25% investment allowance. A similar allowance of 15% is granted on the cost of a new factory or hotel building. Expenditure on factory or hotel buildings may be written off in ten years whilst an allowance of R1,000 is available to any business in respect of each house constructed for its employees.

125% of all costs incurred in the training of local citizens can be offset for tax purposes where the training consists of course attendance at a recognised institution or is provided by a specially recruited full-time training officer.

Tax Incentives—Special

In order to encourage economic and social development in certain fields, a development approval order may be made under which extra tax reliefs on revenue or capital account will be granted for specific business development projects if the Minister is satisfied that such projects are beneficial to Botswana. In considering an application for a development approval order, the Minister will have regard to proposals bearing on:

a. the employment and training of citizens;
b. the localisation of employment positions;
c. the participation by citizens in management and investment in the business; and
d. the locality of the development project and its effect on general economic advancement, pace levels and social conditions.

In the case of any major industrial or commercial business of outstanding importance to the development of Botswana a special tax agreement may be drawn up. This allows the Government the flexibility of either lowering or raising the tax payable by a company, as was the case with the mining companies.

Company Tax and Other Tax Considerations

Company tax is 30%, which is the lowest in Southern Africa. The Income Tax Act 1973 provides for a withholding tax of 15% on dividend and interest payments outside the country. This is designed to induce investors to reinvest their profits in Botswana.

Industrial production in Botswana. Under the Industrial Licensing Act (1968) all manufacturing establishments either employing over nine workers, or using 25 HP or more, must be licensed. In April, 1973, there were 28 licensed enterprises.

Most recent statistics indicate that the contribution of manufacturing to G.D.P. is approximately R8 million, of which nearly 80% is derived from the operations of the Botswana Meat Commission.

The commodities manufactured in Botswana are:

a. bags,
b. bread,
c. caps and helmets,
d. cloth, and
e. clothing.

Appendix C. Business Basics

1. Land

General

There are three categories of land in Botswana—State land, Tribal land and freehold land—but it should be noted that freehold title is seldom granted. Subject to satisfying town and country planning requirements land for business purposes can be made available in all categories. At the present time most business activities are centered in the four commercial towns, namely, Lobatse, Gaborone, Selibe-Pikwe and Francistown which are on State land, but it is Government's policy to encourage business development in the Tribal areas, especially in the major villages which in many ways offer very good prospects.

Tenure

Except for existing freehold land, and in certain cases where industrial/commercial land may be available on lease-hold terms, all State land is disposed of in terms of a fixed period State grant which may be considered as a form of

---

Appendix C reprinted from "If You Want to Start a Business in Botswana," published by the Ministry of Commerce and Industry.

limited freehold title. Under this system the State sells the land to an applicant for a specified number of years, and during that period the holder, subject to having complied with an initial development covenant, is in a position of ownership and amongst other things may sell or lease it. At the end of the period, however, the land and all fixed improvements on it will revert to the State without compensation unless the State agrees to make a further grant. The period of a grant depends partly on how it will be developed out—50 years is fairly common. The price of land is based on the replacement cost of installing services plus an additional element of cross subsidy to assist in developing low-cost housing areas.

In the tribal areas land is controlled by the Land Boards who, subject to Presidential consent, are empowered to make land grants. Where a board has not fully developed its industrial area, when considering applications it will normally seek the advice of the Departments of Town and Regional Planning on sitting pending the establishment of its own industrial area. At present the terms on which land can be obtained vary from one Board to another but standard leases are being prepared.

Availability—Commercial Towns

Gaborone (population 34,000)

The original industrial area is a mixture of State land and freehold land and plots vary in size between 1,200 square meters (m²) to 2 hectares (ha.). With few exceptions all State land is occupied but freehold land may become available by private treaty.

The basic land value is approximately R20,000–R25,000 per hectare. A second industrial/commercial estate is being developed by the Botswana Development Corporation (BDC) at Broadhurst next to the Francistown Road. Fully-serviced plots ranging in size from 1,200 m² to 3 ha. can be leased for between one and twenty-five years at a rental of R0.25/m^2 per year increasing by four per cent per year. In certain cases land can be obtained on terms akin to the fixed period state grant, and factory shells are also available. Inquiries should be directed to Martin Heymann and Co. (Botswana) (Pty.) Ltd.

The main commercial area is the Mall but other commercial areas exist near the railway station, in "White City" and in the village. No vacant plots are available but shop and office space may be leased. A new mall and other commercial areas are being developed in the Broadhurst extension of Gaborone and sites will soon be available in two areas which are already serviced.

Owing to an unexpected high rate of expansion the demand for serviced residential land has outstripped the supply and prices have escalated. Recently, however, a large number of plots have become available. High-cost residential plots, which are fully serviced, are currently priced at about R2,500 for a plot of 1,200 m^2, and medium-cost plots are somewhat cheaper. Vacant plots are not available in low-cost areas, but traditional and site-and-service housing areas are being opened up for people in the lower income groups.

Francistown (population 25,000)

There are two main industrial/commercial areas in Francistown, namely, the Dumela Industrial Estate and the Central Industrial Area. The Dumela Industrial Estate was laid out by the town council on level land five kilometres north of the town and adjacent to the railway line. It caters to light and heavy industry; soil conditions are not ideal but rail serviced sites could be provided. Plots range from 1,200 m^2 upwards and can be leased from the town council at R6,200/ha. The Central Industrial Area in the centre of town is mostly State land and is mainly for light industry. Non-rail serviced plots of 1,200 m^2 and larger presently cost about R16,000/ha. It would be possible to develop three rail-serviced plots. A small amount of land is owned by the Tati Company to whom separate application should be made.

There is no State commercial land for disposal but a new area which will border on the present commercial centre and will be developed partly by Government and partly by the Tati Company is in the final planning stage. Commercial land may be obtained by private treaty.

Much new development is underway in Francistown and a new high-cost residential area, which should be ready within a few months, will relieve the present shortage of residential land. House prices are somewhat lower than in Gaborone.

Selebi-Pikwe (population 23,000)

Most of the industrial estate is occupied but a small number of plots are still available including a few which are rail serviced. An extension to the estate is being considered. The main commercial area is in the central Mall which is being developed by the Botswana Development Corporation and there is still plenty of room for expansion. Plots are also available for small businesses in small neighbourhood shopping centres. High- and medium-cost residential plots are currently available and new areas are being prepared for low-cost housing. All land in Selebi-Pikwe costs between R15,000–R20,000/ha.

Lobatse (population 15,000)

A new industrial area has been surveyed but services are still incomplete and plots are therefore not yet on sale. Private purchase of freehold plots may be possible. No State-owned commercial plots are available but a number of privately-owned freehold plots are available for which planning permission for commercial development might be given. At present high-cost residential plots are readily obtainable. The cost of land in Lobatse is considerably lower than in Gaborone and is approximately R8,500/ha.

Availability—Major Villages

Some of these are also tribal capitals and form some of the largest towns in the country, the main examples being Maun (15,000), Serowe (23,000), Palapye (6,000), Tonota/Shashe (7,000), Mahalapye (13,500), Mochudi (14,500), Molepolole (15,000), Ramotswa (9,000), and Kanye (16,000) (all figures estimated for 1975).

These villages and their surrounding areas offer growing business opportunities and steps are being taken to improve their infrastructure. Communications are being improved and in each an area is being set aside for industrial/commercial use. One village, Mochudi, has already developed the Pilane Industrial Estate which is close to the main railway and where plots may be leased from the Kgatleng Land Board.

Further Information

Inquiries for State land should be addressed to the Department of Surveys and Lands who will also assist with information on land matters generally. Inquiries for Tribal land should be addressed to the secretary of the land board concerned. Inquiries in respect to town planning should be made to the Department of Town and Regional Planning.

2. Buildings

Almost all property development for resale or rent is confined to the four commercial towns with the exception of a limited amount of activity by the Botswana Housing Corporation at Maun, Kasane and Serowe.

Housing

The largest property developer is the Botswana Housing Corporation (BHC) which owns and manages most of the housing formerly belonging to Government as well as its own housing and that of other statutory bodies and one local authority. The BHC builds houses at all income levels i.e. high- , medium- , and low-cost, and such housing is available for sale or to rent by public servants and the general public alike.

The Botswana Development Corporation (BDC) is currently erecting 40 mixed design high-cost housing units on the north side of Gaborone and occasionally a small investor puts up a house or flats as an investment.

The biggest constraint in the housing sector is the lack of serviced land. Apart from the BHC most units are built either for company housing or for individuals. Thus there is a severe shortage of housing of all kinds, especially in Gaborone, which is expected to continue for some years, and housing is therefore expensive.

Commercial and Industrial Building

In the main commercial areas, office accommodation and shop space are frequently combined in large blocks erected by private developers.

Premises for factories, wholesale depots, etc., in the industrial/commercial areas are normally erected by the investor himself, but it is possible occasionally to rent or purchase premises from an existing owner. The BDC is prepared to erect factory shells on its Broadhurst Estate in Gaborone by arrangement with the investor.

Costs

As at March, 1976, the approximate cost per square meter (m^2) of various types of accommodation in Gaborone is set out in the table below. Broadly speaking building costs are similar in all four commercial towns but rentals vary as indicated in the table.

Type of Accommodation	To Build	To Lease Monthly
Simple factory/warehouse	R50–R75	R0.95–R1.20
(Rentals approximately the same elsewhere.)		
Housing, high-/medium-cost	R130–R170	R1.50–R3.50
(Rentals approximately similar in Selebi-Pikwe, cheaper elsewhere.)		
Flats	R130–R150	R1.50–R2.50
(Rentals approximately similar in Selebi-Pikwe, cheaper elsewhere.)		R3.00–R4.70
Multi-storey Office accommodation, shops, Retail.	R165–R225	R4.80–R5.40
(Rentals for offices and shops generally cheaper elsewhere.)		

Further information may be obtained from the Botswana Housing Corporation, the Botswana Development Corporation and Martin Heymann and Co. (Botswana) (Pty.) Ltd.

3. Public Utilities

Electricity

Owing to the large distances involved and the low density of population in most of the semi-urban areas electricity supplies are still organised on a town or regional basis and are not yet in the form of a national grid.

In Gaborone and Lobatse and certain adjacent areas electricity is supplied by the Botswana Power Corporation (BPC) from the Gaborone power station (Southern Division) which uses both steam and diesel generators. The BPC also supplies power at Selebi-Pikwe (Northern Division) from the new power station using coal from Morupule Colliery and water from the Shashe Dam. In Francistown power is supplied in bulk by the BPC from Selebi-Pikwe and is distributed by the municipality. Ultimately it is intended to join up the Gaborone and Selebi-Pikwe networks but this is not expected to take place until the mid-1980s.

With the exception of very limited supplies at Maun, Palapye and Mahalapye there are no public power supplies in other centres and many persons and firms have their own private generators. A study has been made of the possibility of providing power to all the main rural centres and implementation is already in progress. Mochudi and the neighbouring Pilane Industrial Estate are already connected, Ramotswa will be connected during 1976 and other centres will be supplied as soon as possible.

The BPC has the same tariff scales for its northern and southern divisions, and Francistown has its own scale. All scales include tariffs for industrial and commercial users which are as follows:

a) *BPC: Business, Commercial and Industrial Tariff Scale* 1–11.0 cents/unit for the first 100 units, 9.0 cents/unit for the next 100 units, and 6.8 cents/unit for the balance of monthly consumption.

   Scale 2—(available only when the estimated monthly maximum demand is not less than 35 kilowatts)—

   A demand charge of R7.40/month per kilowatt of half-hourly maximum demand subject to a minimum charge of R200/month, plus 4.0 cents/unit for all units of monthly consumption.

b) *BPC: Industrial—High Voltage Supplies Tariff*

   A demand charge of R6.60/month per kilowatt of half-hourly maximum demand subject to a minimum charge of R200/month, plus 3.6 cents/unit for all units of monthly consumption.

c) *Francistown: Industrial Use*

   8 cents/unit of the first 1,000 units of monthly consumption, 6 cents/unit for the next 1,000 units and 5 cents/unit for the balance of monthly consumption.

Further information may be obtained from the Botswana Power Corporation and Francistown Town Council.

4. Taxation

The principal law on taxation in Botswana is the Income Tax Act, 1973, now published as Cap. 52:01. Tax is deducted from taxable income which is determined as follows:

Gross income (Part IV, Division II of the Act)
less any amounts exempt from tax
equals Assessable income (Part V)
less cost of producing the assessable income
equals Chargeable income (Part VI)
less Personal allowances (individuals only)
equals Taxable income (Part VII).

Note: For companies taxable income is the same as chargeable income.

Individuals

Rates of Tax are set out in the Tenth Schedule of the Act:

		Taxable Income		*Rate of Tax*
a)	Resident:	first	R 600	10%
		next	R 2,000	15%

Taxable Income			Rate of Tax
next	R	1,000	20%
next	R	1,000	30%
next	R	2,000	40%
next	R	3,000	50%
next	R	8,000	60%
next	R	8,000	70%
exceeding	R	25,600	75%
b) Non-resident:	all taxable income		20%

Personal Allowances (Section 47 of the Act)

A married person is entitled to a personal allowance of R2,400 and an unmarried person to a personal allowance of R1,200.

Wife's Income (Section 60 of the Act)

Although a wife's income is deemed to accrue to her husband relief is given in the case of a resident so that any employment income of his wife (but not including any such income received from her husband) is taxed as if the wife were an unmarried person.

Companies

All companies operating in Botswana, whether resident or non-resident, are charged tax at the rate of 35% of their taxable income. Allowances in respect to various types of expenditure are granted as follows:

Industrial Buildings (Third Schedule, Parts I and II)

a) *New*—total equals 115%, 15% being an investment allowance in the year of first use, and 100% being an annual allowance granted at rate of 10% per year for ten years.

b) *Used*—total equals 100% being an annual allowance granted at the rate of 10% per year for ten years.

c) *Improvements (not repairs) to either (a) or (b)*—total equals 115%, 15% being an investment allowance in the year when the improvements were completed, and 100% being an annual allowance granted at the rate of 10% per year for ten years.

Plant and Machinery (Third Schedule, Parts I and II)

d) *New or unused*—total equals 125% being an investment allowance granted in the year of first use, and 100% being an annual allowance granted at whatever rate the investor chooses provided that the total allowed shall be not more than the total relevant expenditure.

e) *Used*—total equals 100% being an annual allowance granted at whatever rate the investor chooses provided that total allowed shall be not more than the total relevant expenditure.

Note: The investment allowance is allowed only to an "approved industrial business" i.e. a business engaged in a process of manufacture or an hotel.

Employees' Housing (Third Schedule, Part III)

An allowance of up to the amounts shown below in respect of each house built to accommodate employees:

Farming—R5,000

Mining—nil (special provision is made in respect of mining).

All other business—R1,000

Training (Section 41 of the Act)

In ascertaining the chargeable income of any company there is deducted an amount equal to 125% of any expenditure incurred during the tax year on approved post-secondary education or training, or on the employment of an approved full-time training officer.

Further tax allowances additional to those set out above

may be granted under a Development Approval Order (Section 52 of the Act) in respect to any business considered to be of special value to the development of Botswana. (Section 54 of the Act of Parliament.)

There is a withholding tax of 15% on interest and dividends paid to non-residents. Double taxation agreements exist with the United Kingdom, South Africa and Sweden. Special provisions exist in respect to farming and mining.

Further information may be obtained from the Commissioner of Taxes.

5. Financial Services

Banking

There are two commercial banks in Botswana, Barclays Bank of Botswana Ltd. and Standard Bank Botswana Ltd., both of which have their head offices in Gaborone and are subsidiaries of international banks based in Britain. Banking facilities are growing rapidly and range from branches providing the full spread of services in the main towns to a network of agencies in the rural areas, some of them so distant that they must be serviced by air. There is no stock exchange in Botswana but arrangements can be made with one of the banks to make a market in the shares of any locally registered public company.

The Post Office Savings Bank operates throughout the country along the same lines as similar institutions elsewhere.

Development Finance

The Botswana Development Corporation (BDC) is a Government-owned public company which was set up in 1970 with the object of stimulating economic development by identifying viable investment opportunities and developing them either on its own or in partnership with other local or foreign investors. The Corporation participates by providing equity capital and/or medium or long-term loans; it also assists in the preparation of market surveys and financial feasibility studies. For the most part it operates on a normal commercial basis but a special section has been set up to handle participation in sub-commercial projects offering particular economic or social benefits. Other financial assistance is available from an associate company (see below).

The BDC's interests are wide-ranging and amongst other things include property development, building and construction, air transport, hotels, insurance, farming, brewing and diamond valuing. Its total net assets as at the end of 1975 were approximately R8 million.

The National Development Bank (NDB) is a parastatal body which was set up in 1964 primarily to provide financial assistance in the agricultural sector, especially to the small farmer. The scope of its lending has widened steadily and it is now also involved in water development, low-cost housing and the industrial and commercial sector. The volume of its lending has also greatly expanded and is now about R2.7 million yet the bank remains committed to its original objective of helping the small man and the majority of its loans are to small farmers and average approximately R350. Small farmers commonly lack conventional security and emphasis has therefore been placed, with success, on providing them with "character" loans. Such loans are made in kind not cash.

The Bank's funds are made available by or through Government on favourable terms which enable the Bank to lend at interest rates lower than those available commercially.

The Financial Services Company of Botswana (Pty.) Ltd. was formed in 1974 by the BDC, NDB and the two commercial banks. To date its activities have been hire-purchase finance, normally for periods in excess of one year, and leasing finance, generally in respect of plant and machinery only although buildings would also be considered as part of a package deal. It is intended in the near future to offer medium-term (5–8 years) loan facilities to individuals wishing to start up new developments, for example new farms, for which there is at present no suitable source of finance.

Insurance

The country's first locally-based insurance company, I.G.I. Botswana Ltd., was formed at the end of 1974, and was followed a year later by the formation of the Botswana Insurance Company Ltd. They are both linked with major overseas companies and are thus able to offer all normal insurance services. There are two insurance brokers, J. H. Minet and Co. (Botswana) (Pty.) Ltd. and Barclays Bank Insurance Division, and several agents.

Building Societies

There is one building society, the United Building Society, with offices in Gaborone, which provides mortgage finance for privately-owned houses up to a ceiling of approximately R20,000.

6. Companies, Trademarks and Other Legislation

The Companies Registry is responsible for the administration of several Acts of Parliament of great importance to businessmen:

a) All companies operating in Botswana must be either incorporated or registered under the Companies Act (Cap. 42:01), according to whether they are local or external companies.

b) The Registration of Business Names Act (No. 14 of 1975) is not yet in force pending the making of regulations but when it comes into operation it will require that any person, other than a firm or company, carrying on business in Botswana under a name which is not his true surname must register his business name and certain other particulars with the Registrar of Business Names.

c) Trade Marks are governed by the Trade Marks Act (Cap. 68:03) and the United Kingdom Trade Marks Act (Cap. 68:04); Patents and Designs are covered by the Patents and Designs Protection Act (Cap. 68:02). In all cases it is provided that only rights granted in either the United Kingdom or South

Africa may be re-registered in Botswana in which case they will be fully protected. No protection is available for rights which have not been granted in one of these countries.

Further information may be obtained from the Companies Registry.

7. Foreign Trade

Southern African Customs Union

Botswana is a member of the Southern African Customs Union, which also includes Lesotho, Swaziland and South Africa and, with the exception of any goods on which Botswana may have imposed a protective duty in terms of Article 6 of the Customs Union Agreement, all trade between Botswana and the other member countries is free of customs and sales duty.

All goods entering Botswana from the areas of the other member countries must still be declared to Customs at the first place of importation but this is only for statistical purposes to enable Botswana to calculate and claim its shares of the Common Customs revenue pool. It should be noted, however, that a limited range of goods from the other member countries may be subject to permit requirements in Botswana, examples being firearms, hides and skins and livestock.

EEC-ACP Convention of Lomé

Botswana is a signatory to the Lomé Convention signed on 28th February, 1975, between the European Economic Community (EEC) and 46 African, Carribean and Pacific states. The Convention, which continues until 1st March, 1980, contains a wide range of most important provisions including the following:

> *Trade:* Unrestricted and duty free access to the EEC market for most of the manufactures and products, including most agricultural products, of the ACP states, on a non-reciprocal basis. Effectively this creates a preferential trading area of some 250 million people. It is important to note that the Community's rules of origin of goods have been specially adapted so that all ACP states are treated for this purpose as a single originating territory.

> *Export Earnings* of the ACP states will be stabilised in respect to certain products the list of which may later be extended.

> *Industrial Corporation:* Various measures will be taken to promote industrial development in the ACP states, including the setting up of a centre for Industrial Development.

> *Financial and Technical Cooperation:* Under this heading a large volume of development aid will be provided to the ACP states from the European Development Fund and the European Investment Bank.

General

Botswana has made or acceded to trade agreements with Zambia, Malawi and Rhodesia; she applied *de facto* the rules of the General Agreement on Tariffs and Trade (GATT); and she benefits under the Generalised System of Preferences (GSP) under which developing countries receive preferential treatment for their export to certain industrial countries.

Import licences are required for a wide range of goods from countries other than those already mentioned above, but in most cases licences are granted freely upon application provided the goods are intended for home consumption in Botswana.

Customs and Excise

All Customs and Excise functions are carried out under the authority of the Customs and Excise Duty Act (Cap. 50:01) as amended from time to time. In effect the Botswana Act and related tariff schedules are identical in their provisions with those of South Africa and the other member countries of the Customs Union.

Apart from their normal range or duties the Department of Customs and Excise carry out two other functions:

a) The issue of certificates of origin for goods produced or manufactured in Botswana.

b) The issue of most import and export licences. The main regulations are contained in the Import Control Notice (Statutory Instrument No. 72 of 1972), but in certain cases additional permits may be required under other regulations.

Botswana Origin

For goods to qualify as being of Botswana origin when exported to the other member countries of the Southern African Customs Union they must comply with the minimum requirements of Section 46 of the Customs and Excise Duty Act (the same provisions apply in the other member countries):

a) at least 25% of the production cost of those goods must be represented by materials produced or labour performed in Botswana;

b) the last process in the production or manufacture of the goods must have taken place in Botswana;

Only the following items may be included in production cost—

    i. the cost to the manufacturer of all materials;

   ii. manufacturing wages and salaries;

  iii. direct manufacturing expenses;

  iv. overhead factory expenses;

   v. the cost of inside containers i.e. the immediate wrappings in which goods are necessarily enclosed;

  vi. other expenses incidental to the manufacturing operation in the discretion of the Director of Customs and Excise.

Note: The question of origin, which may well affect the amount of import duty payable on goods, is determined by the authorities of the importing country, not the exporting country. Many countries have different regulations from Botswana and inquiries should be addressed to the authorities, normally Customs, in the country to which goods are intended to be exported.

Further information may be obtained from the Ministry of Commerce and Industry and the Department of Customs and Excise.

8. Licensing Requirements

Manufacturing Industry

With few exceptions all manufacturing industries which employ ten or more persons including directors and/or use engines providing energy totalling not less than 25 horsepower must have an industrial licence issued under the Industrial Development Act (Cap. 43:01). Each licence must be renewed annually but renewal is automatic provided the goods specified in the licence continue to be manufactured. The fee is R100 per year.

All applications for industrial licences must be published in two consecutive issues of the *Government Gazette* and the *Daily News*. Any person may object to the granting of an application on the grounds, detailed in Section 10 of the Act, that the proposed activity would be harmful to the development of the country, the industry, or, if he is himself a licensed manufacturer in the industry, to his own business. Such investigations will then be made as are necessary to establish the facts on which a decision can be taken.

In exceptional cases, e.g. where the investment requirement is very large, an exclusive licence may be granted which prohibits the setting up of any competing industry in Botswana. Such licences may be granted for a maximum of four years in the first instance but may be extended for one further period of up to four years.

Application forms can be obtained from the Ministry of Commerce and Industry, Industrial Section, and it is wise to contact them at an early stage in the planning of a venture.

Internal Trade

The principal legislation governing trade in Botswana is the Trading Act (Cap. 43:02) as amended. It is important to note that whereas the term "trade" is defined as meaning "to carry on the business of selling goods" the Act also applies to several activities where only services are sold, e.g. travel agent, driller.

A wide range of activities require to be licensed, either by the national licensing authority (town or district council). Licence fees are very reasonable and in only one case (banker) does a fee exceed R100. Examples of fees are:

General Trading	R100
Small General Trading	R 20
Wholesaler	R 80
External representative:	
resident	R 20
non-resident	R100

Although not concerned with licensing mention should be made of a number of other measures affecting trade. Prices generally are subject to the Control of Goods (Trading Margins) (No. 2) Regulations, 1974 (Statutory Instrument No. 146 of 1974), as amended, but the prices of petroleum and sugar are each controlled by separate regulations made under the Control of Goods Act, 1973. To assist the consumer prices must be properly displayed as required by the Control of Goods (Marketing of Goods) Regulations, 1974 (Statutory Instrument No. 121 of 1974), and quantities must be indicated clearly as laid down in the Weights and Measures (Sales of Articles) Regulations, 1973 (Statutory Instrument No. 38 of 1973). The hours during which shops may be open for business are regulated under the Shop House Act (Cap. 43:04).

Further information may be obtained from the Ministry of Commerce and Industry, Commercial Section or from town and district councils.

Weights and Measures

Although no licence is required it is essential that all equipment concerned with weighing and measuring for purposes of trade should be accurate and should be regularly assized as required by the Weights and Measures Act (Cap. 43:06) and regulations made under it.

The only legal system of weights and measures in Botswana is the metric S.I. system.

Further information may be obtained from the Division of Weights and Measures.

Index